THE NAMES OF JESUS

Books by Vincent Taylor

*

Speaker's Lectures

THE LIFE AND MINISTRY OF JESUS

THE PERSON OF CHRIST IN NEW TESTAMENT TEACHING

*

THE FORMATION OF THE GOSPEL TRADITION

JESUS AND HIS SACRIFICE

FORGIVENESS AND RECONCILIATION

THE GOSPEL ACCORDING TO ST. MARK

THE CROSS OF CHRIST

THE NAMES OF JESUS

BY

VINCENT TAYLOR

PH.D., D.D. (LOND.), HON. D.D. (LEEDS), HON. D.D. (DUBLIN),
HON. D.D. (GLASGOW), F.B.A.

FORMERLY PRINCIPAL AND FERENS TUTOR IN NEW TESTAMENT LANGUAGE AND
LITERATURE AT WESLEY COLLEGE, HEADINGLEY, LEEDS

LONDON

MACMILLAN & CO LTD

NEW YORK · ST MARTIN'S PRESS

1959

First Edition 1953
Reprinted 1954, 1959

MACMILLAN AND COMPANY LIMITED
London Bombay Calcutta Madras Melbourne

THE MACMILLAN COMPANY OF CANADA LIMITED
Toronto

ST MARTIN'S PRESS INC
New York

PRINTED IN GREAT BRITAIN

PREFACE

THIS work, which consists of a study of the Names of Jesus, forms the First Series of the Speaker's Lectures delivered at Oxford during the years 1951-2. It will be followed, it is hoped, by a Second Series on 'Jesus of Nazareth: His Life and Ministry', and a Third on 'The Person of Christ in New Testament Teaching'. Hitherto the first of these subjects has not, I believe, been treated in detail, although every work on the Person of Christ rightly devotes careful attention to the principal names and titles. It is important, however, to examine as many names as possible, and to cast the net widely, including phrases which might perhaps be regarded as descriptive rather than as names proper. For reasons stated in the Introduction these designations have a special claim upon the attention of the student, and particularly before the larger questions are examined in detail. The inquiry is far more than an intellectual exercise, especially when the Biblical doctrine of the Incarnation is in question. Such studies can be fruitfully pursued only if the mind is first steeped in the actual teaching of the Gospels, the Acts, the Epistles, and the Apocalypse, and even then only if the various influences, devotional, liturgical, catechetical, and doctrinal, out of which the teaching emerges, are fully appraised. It is in this persuasion that the present Lectures were written and delivered.

Studies of names and titles demand scrupulous regard to detail. Many years ago this truth was deeply impressed on my mind by a trenchant passage in Harnack's *Sayings of Jesus*. In the Preface of that work (p. xiif) Harnack speaks sarcastically of the way men soar away into sublime discussions concerning the meaning of 'the Kingdom of God', 'the Son of Man', 'Messiahship', and other problems, 'while the "lower" problems, whose treatment involves real scavenger's labour, in which one is almost choked with dust, are passed by on the other side'. 'Hence', he says, 'the wretched plight in which the criticism of the gospels finds itself in these days, and indeed has always found itself – with the exception of the work of a few critics, and apart from the Markan problem, which has been treated with scientific thoroughness'. I doubt if these charges were ever relevant as regards British research, but they are worth recalling to-day when there is a temptation to enter too quickly into the realms of Biblical theology and to be intoxicated by the lure of Typology. Having spent a considerable part of my life as 'a scavenger' among 'the dust', I can heartily endorse Harnack's warning. I do not think we are likely to make much progress in criticism and theology if we elect to be black-coated workmen. We must certainly have the insight and the imagination to discern the larger issues, but we are least likely to be betrayed by the creative urge if we have first patiently collected and sat down before the basic facts.

I hope that what is here presented may be of interest and profit to students, but I must also confess that I am not without hope that students who are also preachers will find in the Names of Jesus moving themes in a day when many hearers of the Word resent pious platitudes and look for instruction in Christian doctrine.

I am greatly indebted to a former colleague, the Rev. Owen E. Evans, M.A., B.D., and to a present colleague, the Rev. Dr. John H. S. Kent, M.A., for the generous help they have given me in the correction of the proofs.

Nov. 30th 1952   VINCENT TAYLOR

CONTENTS

CONTENTS

ABBREVIATIONS

Billerbeck   = *Kommentar zum NT aus Talmud und Midrasch*,
            H. L. Strack und P. Billerbeck.

EB   = *Encyclopaedia Biblica.*

ET   = *The Expository Times.*

Exp. Gk. Test = *The Expositor's Greek Testament.*

JBL   = *The Journal of Biblical Literature.*

JTS   = *The Journal of Theological Studies.*

KThW   − *Theologisches Wörterbuch*, ed. G. Kittel.

TWB   = *A Theological Word Book of the Bible*, ed. A.
            Richardson.

VGT   = *The Vocabulary of the Greek Testament*, J. H.
            Moulton and G. Milligan.

ZThK   = *Zeitschrift f. Theol. und Kirche.*

INTRODUCTION

THE modern practice of beginning a study of the Person of Christ with the Names of Jesus is not without good reason. Many of these names have a history and all serve the ends of interpretation. We can consider their original and their contemporary meaning, and examine how they are used by Jesus Himself and by the New Testament writers. They supply, therefore, a welcome note of objectivity in an investigation in which much must be inferential and at times speculative. Further, they carry us back to a time when doctrinal motives were only beginning to be operative, long before the period of more formal discussion during the second to the fifth centuries. They throw light upon the primitive Christian tradition, on which St. Paul, the writer of the Epistle to the Hebrews, and St. John drew, and which they developed in various ways; and they disclose a ferment of Christological reflection in Jewish Christianity, as well as in Gentile communities of the Greek world. Again, the various names enable us to trace the history of Christological thinking, since they indicate views which persisted into later times, and other estimates which fell by the way side because they proved to be immature and inadequate. In short, the names of Jesus are both the foreshadowing and the precipitate of Christology in its beginnings; they anticipate developments and reveal what Christians thought in the creative period of theology. The question, who Jesus is, is approached best by considering how men named Him, for it is by His names that He is revealed and known.

PART ONE

THE PRINCIPAL NAMES
AND TITLES OF JESUS

I

JESUS

OF all names none is more precious in Christian ears than the name 'Jesus'.[1] From the end of the first century it expressed a deepseated Christian sentiment of veneration and worship. In itself, however, it is a personal name significant by reason of its meaning. It transcribes the Greek Ἰησοῦς, which was used for the Hebrew *Jeshua*, a shortened form of *Jehoshua* (Joshua), 'He whose salvation is Yahweh', or, more briefly, 'God's salvation'.

In the first century the name was by no means uncommon. Josephus mentions about twenty persons so named, ten of whom were contemporaries of Jesus Himself, and at the end of the first century and the beginning of the second the name is freely found in Egyptian papyri, ostraca, and inscriptions.[2] A striking change, however, is manifest from the second century onwards. Henceforward, the name 'Jesus' was abandoned by Jews by reason of antagonism to Christianity, and was avoided by Christians from motives of reverence. As Deissmann points out,[3] this tendency can be traced in the textual

---

[1] *Dulcis memoria Jesu.*

[2] Cf. *VGT*, 301f.; Deissmann, *Mysterium Christi*, 7–11 ; Foerster, *KThW*, iii, 284–94.

[3] *Mysterium Christi*, 15-26. Copyists tended to alter the name when it was used of other persons. See the variants in the Lukan Genealogy (Lk. iii. 29); in Mt. xxvii. 16f. in the reading 'Jesus Barabbas'; in Ac. vii. 45 (Joshua) and xiii. 6 (Bar-Jesus). It is possible also that the name originally stood in Mk. xv. 7 with reference to Barabbas, and in Philm. 24 between 'Christ' and 'Mark'. Deissmann, *op. cit.*, 17f., points out that the Old Latin Pauline text omitted the words *et Iesus qui dicitur* in Col. iv. 11.

tradition. 'Clearly', he says, 'it was felt to be a scandal, and that in early times, that there should have been other men of the name *Jesus*, especially men who for certain reasons were repugnant to Christian sentiment'.[1]

In the Evangelists' use of the name there is a remarkable degree of objectivity; only in Mt. i. 21[2] is it a cult-name. How frequently the name appears is shown by the fact that in Moulton and Geden's *Concordance* nearly twelve columns are needed to record the examples, and of these more than four and a half columns belong to the Fourth Gospel. In five cases ὁ Ναζωραῖος[3] is added and ὁ Ναζαρηνός[4] is found six times. In contrast with 'Jesus', the name 'Jesus Christ' is extremely rare. There are only two certain examples in the Synoptic Gospels,[5] and two more in Jn.[6] 'Christ Jesus' and 'Our Lord Jesus Christ' are never used, and 'Lord Jesus' appears nowhere except once in the spurious ending of Mk[7] and in a doubtful reading in Lk. xxiv. 3. A comparison with the Acts and the Epistles will show how primitive the usage of the Gospels is, including that of the Fourth Gospel, reflecting as they do the conditions which belong to the historic ministry and not that of the period of composition.

The Acts reveals an interesting transition to fuller forms of expression. The name 'Jesus' is still found more frequently than any other. Harnack[8] says that it is

---

[1] *Op. cit.*, 16.

[2] 'Thou shalt call his name Jesus; for it is he that shall save his people from their sins'.

[3] Mt. xxvi. 71, Lk. xviii. 37, Jn. xviii. 5, 7, xix. 19. Cf. Mt. ii. 23.

[4] Mk. i. 24, x. 47, xiv. 67, xvi. 6, Lk. iv. 34, xxiv. 19.

[5] Mk. i. 1, Mt. i. 1. In Mt. i. 18 B reads 'Christ Jesus'.

[6] Jn. i. 17 (the Prologue) and xvii. 3 (the highpriestly prayer).

[7] Mk. xvi. [19], where, however, 'the Lord' should probably be read as in xvi. [20].

[8] *The Date of the Acts and the Synoptic Gospels*, 104.

used thrce times as often as the name 'Christ'. Ναζωραῖος[1]
is used seven times. But the terms 'Lord Jesus',[2] 'Jesus
Christ',[3] 'the Lord Jesus Christ',[4] 'Our Lord Jesus
Christ',[5] and 'Christ Jesus'[6] are manifestly coming
into favour. One sees a strong primitive tendency
and a desire for richer devotional forms going hand in
hand.

In the rest of the New Testament, and particularly in
the Pauline, Catholic, and Pastoral Epistles,[7] the names
'Jesus Christ', 'Christ Jesus', and 'the Lord Jesus Christ'
are used with the greatest frequency. It is remarkable,
however, how often the name 'Jesus' appears in the Pauline letters, being found at least eighteen times.[8] As
early as Phil. ii. 10 there is a distinct religious tone in the
phrase, 'that in the name of Jesus every knee should bow'.
In the Epistle to the Hebrews the same emphasis is seen
in the manner in which the writer holds back the personal
name, 'generally', as Moffatt says, as 'the climax of an
impressive phrase or phrases'.[9] In the Apocalypse[10] also,
and in I Jn,[11] there are striking phrases which preserve the
recollection of the historical Jesus.

In general, we may say that the name 'Jesus' is used in

---

[1] Ac. ii. 22, iii. 6, iv. 10, vi. 14, xxii. 8, xxiv. 5, xxvi. 9.

[2] Ac. i. 21, iv. 33, vii. 59, viii. 16, xi. 20, xv. 11, xvi. 31, xix. 5, 13, 17,
xx. 21, 24, 35, xxi. 13.

[3] Ac. ii. 38, iii. 6, iv. 10, viii. 12, ix. 24, x. 36, 48, xvi. 18.

[4] Ac. xi. 17, xxviii. 31.

[5] Ac. xv. 26.

[6] Ac. iii. 20, v. 42, xvii. 3, xxiv. 24.

[7] For the Pastoral and Catholic Epistles see p. 22.

[8] Rom. iii. 26, viii. 11, x. 9; 1 Cor. xii. 3 (bis); 2 Cor. iv. 5, 10 (bis),
11 (bis), 14, xi. 4; Gal. vi. 17; Eph. iv. 21; Phil. ii. 10; 1 Thess. i. 10
iv 14 (bis).

[9] Heb., lxiii. Cf. Heb. ii. 9, iii. 1, iv. 14, vi. 20, vii. 22, x. 19, xii. 2, 24,
xiii. 12, 20.

[10] Apoc. i. 9 (bis). xii. 17, xiv. 12, xvii. 6, xix. 10 (bis), xx. 4, xxii. 16.

[11] 1 Jn. i. 7, ii. 22, iv. 3, v. 1, 5.

the New Testament where the narrative interest is upper-
most or where it is desired to emphasize the humanity
of the Lord. The first Christians could never forget that
the grace of God had been manifested to them in His
human personality. In his own idiom, the Fourth
Evangelist expressed a treasured conviction of primitive
Christianity when he wrote: 'And the Word became
flesh, and tabernacled among us, and we beheld his glory,
glory as of the only begotten of the Father, full of grace
and truth' (i. 14). At the same time it would be wrong to
suppose, especially in the Epistles, that when the New
Testament writers used the name 'Jesus', they were
guided only by historical realism. From a very early
point a religious quality attached itself to the name, just
as in later Christianity it belongs even to the pronouns
'He' and 'Him'. In many cases we cannot fail to be
conscious of this nuance, even though proof is not possible.
The well-known words attributed to St. Bernard of
Clairvaux represent an inevitable development which is
rooted in the New Testament itself: 'The name of Jesus
is both light and nourishment. . . . As honey to the taste,
as melody in the ear, as songs of gladness in the heart,
so is the name of Jesus. And medicine it is as well. . . .
Naught but the name of Jesus can restrain the impulse of
anger, repress the swelling of pride, cure the wound of
envy, bridle the onslaught of luxury, extinguish the flame
of carnal desire – can temper avarice, and put to flight
impure and ignoble thoughts. For when I name the name
of Jesus, I call to mind at once a Man meek and lowly of
heart, benign, pure, temperate, merciful; a Man con-
spicuous for every honourable and saintly quality; and
also in the same Person the Almighty God – so that He
both restores me to health by His example and renders
me strong by His assistance. No less than this is

brought to my mind by the name of Jesus whenever I
hear it'.[1]

[1] *in cant. sermo* 43. 4, 5. Cited by K. E. Kirk, *The Vision of God*, 356.
The text is from Cant. i. 13 (Vulg. i. 12).

II
THE SON OF JOSEPH;
THE SON OF MARY

ALTHOUGH few in number, the references to Jesus as 'the Son of Joseph' bear striking testimony to the fidelity of the Evangelists to the earliest tradition. Two of these examples appear in Lk, in the opening words of the Genealogy, in iii. 23, 'being the son (as was supposed) of Joseph', and in the question of the people of Nazareth in iv. 22, 'Is not this Joseph's son?'. Two more are found in Jn, in the words of Philip in i. 45, 'Jesus of Nazareth, the son of Joseph', and the question of the Jews in vi. 42, 'Is not this Jesus, the son of Joseph, whose father and mother we know?'. Joseph is also mentioned ten times in the Birth Stories of Mt and Lk, and there are five allusions to the 'parents' of Jesus in Lk. ii, in the phrases 'the parents' (27), 'his parents' (41 and 43), 'his father and his mother' (33), and the words of Mary, Your father and I sought you sorrowing' (48). It is also possible, and even probable, that the Matthean Genealogy ended originally with the words, 'And Joseph begat Jesus, who is called Christ' (Mt. i. 16).[1] Whatever problems these passages may raise, the phrases bear unimpeachable testimony to the reality of the humanity of Jesus.

The only reference to Jesus as 'the son of Mary' appears in Mk. vi. 3, 'Is not this the carpenter, the son of Mary?', as the text is usually read. Two passages contain the phrase 'Mary his mother' (Mt. ii. 11 and Lk. ii. 34).

---

[1] See the discussion of Mt. i. 16 in my *Historical Evidence for the Virgin Birth* (1920), pp. 105-14. The verb is used of legal descent.

Jn. xix. 25f. refers to her three times, without name, as 'his mother', and Ac. i. 14 mentions her as 'Mary the mother of Jesus'.[1] Like the references to Joseph, the allusions to Mary attest the reality of the birth of Jesus. The solitary instance, however, of the name 'the Son of Mary' (Mk. vi. 3) is open to question on grounds of text and usage.[2] Probably, it is a gloss in the interests of the doctrine of the Virgin Birth, in a text which originally was more akin to the parallel passage in Mt. xiii. 55, 'Is not this the carpenter's son? is not his mother called Mary?'. All the more remarkable is the way in which this name came to establish itself in the language of Christian devotion. The last line in the hymn, 'When our heads are bowed with woe', altered through doctrinal prejudice into the incongruous words, 'Jesu, Son of David, hear', has been restored in most modern hymnbooks to its original form, 'Jesu, Son of Mary, hear'.

[1] In all her name appears nineteen times in the New Testament.

[2] In *The Gospel according to St. Mark*, 299f., I have discussed this reading and the testimony of Origen, that Jesus is nowhere called 'the carpenter' in the Gospels.

III

RABBI; RABBONI; TEACHER; MASTER

THESE four names may with advantage be taken together.

'Rabbi' means literally 'My great one', and 'Rabboni' is an intensified form of the word.[1] Both are terms of respect addressed to teachers of the Law. F. C. Burkitt suggests that the nearest English equivalent is 'Sir'.[2] In the Gospels 'Rabboni' is found twice only: in Mk. x. 51[3] (the cry of Bartimaeus), and in Jn. xx. 16 (by Mary Magdalene). 'Rabbi' is used in Mk three times: in ix. 5 and xi. 21 by Peter, and in xiv. 45 by Judas. Apart from the saying, 'Be not you called Rabbi' (xxiii. 7f.), Mt has only one additional example, in the question of Judas, 'Is it I, Rabbi?' (xxvi. 25).[4] Lk does not use the word, but Jn has it eight times.[5]

'Teacher' is much the more common term in the Synoptics. Of twenty-four examples of διδάσκαλος nineteen are in the vocative.[6] These, with the remaining five, show that during His ministry Jesus was spoken of as 'the Teacher'. This custom is suggested by Mk. v. 35, where the servants of Jairus protest, 'Why trouble the

---

[1] Cf. Dalman, *Jesus-Jeshua*, 13; Black, *An Aramaic Approach to the Gospels and Acts*, 21.

[2] *Christian Beginnings*, 42f.

[3] 'Jesus, Rabbi' is read by D a b ff i sy[8].

[4] In xxvi. 49 Mt has a parallel to Mk. xiv. 45.

[5] Jn. i. 38, 49, iii. 2, 26, iv. 31, vi. 25, ix. 2, xi. 8.

[6] Ten are in Mk: iv. 38, ix. 17, 38, x. 17, 20, 35, xii. 14, 19, 32, xiii. 1. Matthew has parallels to three of these, and Luke to five. Cf. also Mt. viii. 19, xii. 38, xxii. 36; Lk. vii. 40, x. 25, xi. 45, xii. 13, xix. 39, xxi. 7.

teacher any further?', and in Mt. ix. 11 and xvii. 24, in
which, in addressing the disciples, the Pharisees and the
collectors of the half-shekel use the phrase, contempt-
uously, 'your teacher'. [Jesus Himself uses the word in
His message to the householder in Jerusalem,]'The
teacher saith, Where is my guest-chamber, where I shall
eat the passover with my disciples?' (Mk. xiv. 14=
Mt. xxvi. 18=Lk. xxii. 11), and in the saying, 'Be not you
called Rabbi: for one is your teacher and all you are
brethren' (Mt. xxiii. 8). More than the teacher-disciple
relationship is suggested by the use of this term, and this
fact is the justification for the RV rendering 'Master'
in Mk. xiv. 14. Luke appears to have felt the inadequacy
of διδάσκαλος, for when the disciples are the speakers he
prefers to use ἐπιστάτης ('Master'), a word which he has
six times.[1] This preference, however, is peculiar to himself. John uses διδάσκαλος twice in the saying, 'You call
me, Teacher, and Lord: and you say well; for so I am.
If I then, the Lord and the Teacher, have washed your
feet, you also ought to wash one another's feet' (xiii. 13f.).[2]
In i. 38 and xx. 16 he explains that διδάσκαλος is the
equivalent of 'Ραββεί and 'Ραββουνεί respectively. In
iii. 2 he describes Nicodemus as saying that Jesus is a
divinely sent διδάσκαλος, and xi. 28 represents Martha
as saying to her sister, 'The Master is here, and calleth
you.' The fact that the RV has 'Master' here illustrates a
sense of strain in the Evangelists' use of διδάσκαλος. In
this respect John is at one with the Synoptists. Indeed,
in using 'Rabbi' eight times and 'Rabboni' once, his
terminology seems more primitive.

In the usage traced we see in miniature a process
illustrated in many of the names and titles of Jesus. A

---

[1] Lk. v. 5, viii. 24, 45, ix. 33, 49, xvii. 13.
[2] Here again the RV 'Master' seems more appropriate.

primitive title becomes subject to strain and disintegration
as the significance of His person is more fully appraised.
Called 'Rabbi' and 'Teacher' in the days of His ministry,
He comes to be viewed by His disciples as 'Master', a
development not provided for in the classical use of
διδάσκαλος.[1] This terminology had no future. Even
Luke's ἐπιστάτης (*Meister*)[2] was of the things that pass,
for not one of the words under consideration is used in
the New Testament outside the Gospels. In the nine-
teenth century, and in certain circles, the name 'The
Master' regained popularity, but generally as an under-
statement dependent on reverence of tone rather than
precision of meaning. Although rooted in the Gospel
tradition, the archaic usage faded away.

[1] In Cl. Gk. the word denotes a teacher of the arts, and in modern Gk.
it means 'schoolmaster'. *VGT*, 158f. In the LXX it is found twice in
Esth. vi. 1 and 2 Macc. i. 10. Cf. Rengstorf, *KThW*, ii, 153.
[2] Cf. Oepke, *KThW*, ii. 619f.

IV

PROPHET : THE PROPHET

THE Synoptic Gospels show that in popular estimation Jesus was looked upon as a prophet. Among
the people of His day some thought He was John
the Baptist risen from the dead, and others described Him
as 'a prophet, as one of the prophets' (Mk. vi. 15=
Lk. ix. 8; Mk. viii. 28=Mt. xvi. 14=Lk. ix. 19).
Jesus Himself implied that He was esteemed as a prophet
when He declared that a prophet is not without honour,
save in his own country, and among his own kin, and in
his own house (Mk. vi. 4=Mt. xiii. 57),[1] and when
ironically He said, 'It cannot be that a prophet perish out
of Jerusalem' (Lk. xiii. 33). Whether He thought of
Himself as a prophet is more open to question, although
He shared the prophet's ecstasy (Lk. x. 21) and insight
(Mk. vii. 29), and had the consciousness of being 'sent'.[2]

Matthew records that at the Entry the multitudes cried,
'This is the prophet, Jesus, from Nazareth of Galilee'
(xxi. 11), and that the Pharisees desisted from the attempt
to arrest Him because the crowds 'took him for a prophet'
(xxi. 46). Luke has additional examples of this popular
estimation (vii. 16, 39), and expressly speaks of Jesus as
'a prophet mighty in deed and word before God and all
the people' (xxiv. 19).

Johannine evidence is parallel to that of the Synoptics.
'Sir', cries the woman of Samaria, 'I perceive that you
are a prophet' (iv. 19). 'Search and see', say the Pharisees

[1] Cf. Also Lk. iv. 24, Jn. iv. 44.
[2] Cf. H. A. Guy, *New Testament Prophecy*, 52-90.

to Nicodemus, 'that out of Galilee ariseth no prophet'
(vii. 52). Questioned about Jesus, the blind man replies,
'He is a prophet' (ix. 17).

A new element, however, is introduced in Jn by the use
of the term 'the prophet'. The Evangelist represents the
Baptist as denying that he is 'the prophet' but says of
Jesus, after the Feeding of the Five Thousand, that when
the people saw this sign, they said, 'This is of a truth the
prophet that cometh into the world' (vi. 14). Similarly
the multitude at Jerusalem declares, 'This is of a truth
the prophet' (vii. 40). In these passages the promise of a
prophet like Moses, in Deut. xviii. 15, [1] is in mind. Here,
as in Ac. iii. 22 and vii. 37, early Christian teaching has
interpreted the Deuteronomic reference to the institution of the order of prophets as a prediction of the coming
of Jesus.[2] It is in favour of this view that, although the
expectation of a particular prophet is found among the
Samaritans, it was not current among the Jews, and that
there is no echo of it in the Synoptics[3] or the Epistles.
The use of the phrase therefore in Jn and the Acts must
be regarded as a limited attempt, in certain circles, at
Christological interpretation, but one which proved
abortive. None the less, the name is of much interest,
for usages which failed are as much to be expected as those
which had greater success. Like the many attempts to
trace events in the life of Jesus to Old Testament prophecies,[4] the use of the term 'the prophet' was guided
by the sound instinct that the coming of Jesus was in the
fulfilment of the purposes of God.

---

[1] 'The Lord thy God will raise up unto thee a prophet from the midst
of thee, of thy brethren, like unto me; unto him ye shall hearken'.

[2] Cf. Jackson and Lake, *The Beginnings of Christianity*, i. 405.

[3] Apart from the reading of B ('the prophet') in Lk. vii. 39.

[4] As for example the passages in Mt introduced by the phrase, 'that it
might be fulfilled which was spoken by the prophet', or its equivalent.

Again, as in the use of the terms 'Rabbi' and 'Teacher', we have in the titles 'Prophet' and 'the Prophet', names which passed out of use because they were felt to be inadequate. Like the prophets of old, Jesus was seen to be filled with the Spirit and to speak the words of God, but unlike them, He left the abiding impression of possessing far more than the prophetic commission. In contrast with the formula, 'Thus saith the Lord', there remained in the memory of the primitive community His majestic 'But I say unto you'.

V

CHRIST

THUS far, the names examined have been personal and vocational. We now turn to a title which originally is Messianic. Χριστός is the verbal adjective used in the LXX to translate the Hebrew *mashiah*, 'anointed', which in different forms was used in the Old Testament of the appointment of kings, the patriarchs, the people, and, above all, of the expected Scion of David through whom, it was believed, God would deliver and rule His people. How strong was the expectation of the Messiah in the days of Jesus is shown by the Psalms of Solomon (*c.* 40 B.C.), and in the Gospels by the description of Simeon in Lk. ii. 25f. and by the importance repeatedly given to the Messiahship of Jesus. It is necessary, therefore, to consider how the title 'Christ' is applied to Jesus in the New Testament.

It is strange that in Mk the name is used only seven times.[1] The first is in the title, 'The beginning of the Gospel of Jesus Christ, the Son of God' (i. 1). Here the name is personal, the Messianic reference being contained (and transcended) in the phrase, 'Son of God'.[2] Two appear in sayings: 'How say the scribes that the Christ is the son of David' (xii. 35), and 'If any man shall say unto you, Lo, here is the Christ; or, Lo, there; believe it not' (xiii. 21). A fourth in ix. 41 is probably due to

---

[1] Omitting 'to be the Christ' in i. 34 which is probably a case of assimilation to Lk. iv. 41. See *The Gospel according to St. Mark*, 181f.

[2] Omitted by many authorities, but probably original. See *The Gospel according to St. Mark*, 152.

18

textual corruption.[1] In the remaining examples the name
is applied to Jesus by Peter (viii. 29), in the question of
Caiaphas (xiv. 61), and by the chief priests in mockery during the Crucifixion (xv. 32). The most significant point in
the record is that there is no case in Mk in which Jesus
directly applies the title to Himself. The same is true
also of Q. In M the only instance in which it appears is
the saying, 'For one is your master, even the Christ'
(Mt. xxiii. 10), and here the reference has every appearance of being an explanatory comment. The six examples
in L[2] resemble those in Mk. In the Birth Stories, relatively to the size of these sections, the title is used more freely.
In Lk. i and ii 'Christ' is found twice,[3] and in Mt. i and ii
five times.[4] In Lk. iii-xxiv, in addition to two examples
taken over from Mk,[5] there is an addition to the Markan
statement that the devils knew Jesus in the phrase 'that he
was the Christ' (iv. 41). Matthew retains four examples
in Mk,[6] and introduces it into his sources seven times.[7]

From this survey it appears that, with the exception of
two post-Resurrection sayings, every instance of Χριστός
in the Synoptic Gospels is used concerning Jesus, and
not by Him, and that the tendency to use this Messianic
title increases in Mt and Lk, and in Mt in particular
Only in Mk. i. 1 and Mt. i. 1, in the phrase 'Jesus Christ',
is the word used as a personal name.[8] In this respect,

[1] The phrase 'because you are Christ's' may, as T. W. Manson suggests,
be a corruption of 'because you are mine', *The Gospel according to St. Mark*,
408.
[2] Lk. xxii. 67, xxiii. 2, 35, 39, xxiv. 26, 46.
[3] Lk. ii. 11, 26.
[4] Mt. i. 1, 16, 17, 18, ii. 4.
[5] Lk. ix. 20, xx. 41.
[6] Mt. xvi. 16, xxii. 42, xxiv. 23, xxvi. 63.
[7] Mt. xi. 2, xvi. 20, 21, xxiv. 5, xxvi. 68, xxvii. 17, 22.
[8] Possibly also in Mt. i. 16, and in Mt. xvi. 21 if 'Jesus Christ' (WH)
is read, instead of 'Jesus'. Cf. McNeile, *Mt*, 244.

as we shall see, there is a notable contrast between the Gospels and the Epistles.

The usage of the Fourth Gospel is of special interest. In nine passages[1] Χριστός is used of the Messiah without reference to Jesus, and in six directly of Him.[2] The Evangelist also uses the name in a Messianic sense twice in i. 17 and xx. 31. Only once, however, does he introduce it into sayings of Jesus, in xvii. 3, where the name is personal rather than Messianic, and a second time by implication in the reply to the woman of Samaria in the words, 'I that speak unto thee am he' (iv. 26, cf. ix. 35-7). Substantially, therefore, his usage agrees with that of the Synoptists.

We are entitled to conclude, on the basis of the evidence, that Jesus did not speak of Himself as 'the Christ'. This silence does not mean that He did not believe Himself to be the Messiah. His use of other titles, 'the Son' and 'the Son of Man', His tacit acceptance of the confession of Peter, and His reply to Caiaphas leave us in no doubt upon this matter.[3] His unwillingness to use the title must mean that He repudiated the current nationalistic expectations associated with it, feeling the need of a name more suited to express the nature of His mission for men. The Christian community felt otherwise; it had no hesitation in speaking of Him as 'the Christ'. On the contrary, in using the title, it joyfully confessed its faith in Him until the extension of the Gentile Mission necessitated a change of terminology. How deepseated this usage was is seen in the fact that the Gospels, as late as A.D. 65–90, still continued to use the name Messianically at a time when in general usage it had come to be little more than a personal designation.

[1] Jn. i. 20, 25, iii. 28, vii. 27, 31, 41b, 42, ix. 22, xii. 34.
[2] Jn. i. 41, iv. 29, vii. 26, 41a, x. 24, xi. 27.
[3] This must be affirmed despite Bultmann's submission to the contrary, *Theologie des Neuen Testaments*, 26-33.

In this development the evidence of the Acts is conservative. Despite its late date (*c.* A.D. 90), it retains the more primitive usage, owing to its use of early Palestinian sources. Harnack expresses surprise in finding how rarely Χριστός appears in this writing. 'In all', he says, 'it occurs only twenty-five times',[1] and he shows that in all save two instances (ix. 34, x. 36), the name is either Messianic or has a formal connotation.

In contrast, St. Paul repeatedly uses Χριστός as a proper name, either alone or in combination with 'Ιησοῦς. Only perhaps in Rom. ix. 5, 'Of whom is the Christ according to the flesh', has it the meaning 'the Messiah', and even here the inference is not certain. J. Weiss also suggests that the titular meaning is possible in Rom. x. 6f., I Cor. x. 4, xv. 22, 2 Cor. iv. 4, v. 10, but in these passages, he says, 'It is only very faintly suggested; even here the feeling prevails that the concept of the Messiah has been changed into a personal reality'.[2] The oldest form, 'Jesus the Christ', he observes, has entirely disappeared. The fullest title St. Paul uses is 'Our Lord Jesus Christ', which was 'in all probability not invented by him, but was taken over from the customary usage of the congregation', that is, the usage of the Hellenistic communities, 'though perhaps, after all, its final origin goes back to the primitive community'.[3] Dr. L. S. Thornton thinks that Χριστός may be used Messianically in I Cor. i. 23, II Cor. i. 5, Eph. v. 25, Col. i. 24, and I Pet. iv. 13.[4] There can be no

---

[1] *The Date of Acts and of the Synoptic Gospels*, 104. In 14 cases (ii. 31, 36, iii. 18, 20, iv. 26, v. 42, viii. 5, ix. 22, xvii. 3 (*bis*), xviii. 5, 28, xxiv. 24, xxvi. 23), he says, it stands alone with the meaning 'the Messiah'; in 11 other instances it appears in the phrase 'Jesus Christ', but in 7 of these (ii. 38, iii. 6, iv. 10, viii. 12, x. 48, xv. 26, xvi. 18) it has 'a formal connotation'. In xi. 17 and xxviii. 31 it is combined with the title κύριος.

[2] *The History of Primitive Christianity*, 457.

[3] *Op. cit.*, 455.

[4] *The Common Life in the Body of Christ*, 34-7, 106, 225.

doubt, however, that in the majority of cases St. Paul and St. Peter use 'Christ' as a personal name.[1]

In the rest of the New Testament there are very few cases in which we can be confident that Χριστός means 'the Messiah'. I Pet. i. 11, I Jn. ii. 22, v. 1, Apoc. xi. 15, xii. 10 are possible examples. Apart from these passages, and perhaps a few others, 'Christ' and 'Jesus Christ' have become personal names in Hebrews, the Pastoral and Catholic Epistles, and the Apocalypse.[2] The same is true of 'Christ Jesus', 'the Lord Jesus Christ', 'Jesus Christ our Lord', and, in the Pastoral Epistles, 'Our Saviour, Christ Jesus' (2 Tim. i. 10; cf. Tit. i. 4, ii. 13, iii. 6), and in many of these cases the atmosphere of veneration is unmistakable. Liturgical usage has played its part in giving these names the character of 'cult-names'.

How did the change from the purely Messianic sense come to pass? Several considerations are relevant. In the Gentile world the term 'Messiah' was meaningless, unless explained, and when explained was felt to be strange. Further, the term was patently inadequate. Jesus was far more than the Christ of Jewish expectations. He was indeed the Messiah, and, if it was a question of disputation with Jews, this thesis could be vigorously maintained, as Justin Martyr's *Dialogue with Trypho* shows. Nevertheless, in Christian belief, the life, death, and resurrection

---

[1] No stress can be laid on the presence or absence of the article before Χριστός, as a comparison of 1 Cor. i. 13, 17, and 23 shows.

[2] In Heb 'Christ' (9 times) and 'Jesus Christ' (3) are personal names, and the same usage is found in 1 Pet ('Christ' (13 times), 'Jesus Christ' (9)), except possibly, as noted above, in 1 Pet. i. 11. The two references in James (i. 1, ii. 1) are also personal, and the same is true of the 32 (including 26 instances of 'Christ Jesus') in the Pastoral Epistles. So in 2 Pet (8), Jude (6), and 1 and 2 Jn (10), except in 1 Jn. ii. 22 and v. 1 (*v. supra*). The names are personal in the Apoc. (i. 1, 2, 5, xx. 4, 6, xxii. 21), but in xi. 15 and xii. 10, the influence of Psa. ii. 2 is perceptible, and, in consequence, there is a Messianic tone.

of Jesus had so greatly enhanced the significance of His person, that better and more descriptive names and titles were needed for preaching and teaching. Again, for the purposes of communal worship, and in the interests of personal devotion in the life of the Church, a richer terminology was necessary. If Jesus was to be invoked, venerated, and worshipped, He must be called 'Lord' and 'Son of God'. The name 'Christ' could survive only by becoming a personal designation, charged with deep religious meaning by reason of its association with these titles.

c

VI

THE SON OF DAVID

LIKE the name 'Christ', 'the Son of David' is a
Messianic title; it describes the Messiah as a human
figure, a national deliverer, under whose leadership,
it was hoped, the ancient promises of God for Israel would
be fulfilled.

In Mk the title is ascribed to Jesus twice only, in the
story of Blind Bartimaeus (x. 47f. = Mt., xx. 30f. =
Lk. xviii. 38f.). In xii. 35-7 Jesus refers to the teaching
of the scribes, that the Christ is the son of David, and asks
how this can be when David calls him Lord. Davidic
descent is not repudiated in this question, but a different
and more spiritual conception of Messiahship is implied.
In Mt there are six additional cases in which the title is
used of Jesus.[1] Lk has no examples, apart from those taken
from Mk. There are none in Jn, and none in the rest
of the New Testament.

It is apparent that occasionally Jesus was greeted by
this title, but that He did not use it Himself or welcome
it. Matthew discloses a special interest in the title, and
the belief that Jesus was the Son of David is reflected in
the Genealogies. Otherwise interest in this designation
quickly died out in primitive Christianity, although St.
Paul records what may be a phrase from an early creed in
the words 'born of the seed of David' (Rom. i. 3). On
Gentile soil the title was without interest or significance,
and other names were preferred, above all, that of Lord.

[1] Mt. i. 1 (the Genealogy), ix. 27 (The Two Blind Men), xii. 23 (the
multitudes), xv. 22 (the Canaanitish Woman), xxi. 9 (the Entry), and
xxi. 15 (the children in the Temple).

24

VII

THE SON OF MAN

I

IN contrast with 'the Christ' and 'the Son of David',
the title 'the Son of Man' is frequently used by Jesus in
sayings found in all the Gospel sources, Q, Mk, M,
and L. It is always used by Him, and not by others of
Him, the only exception being Ac. vii. 56, in the words of
Stephen, 'Behold, I see the heavens opened, and the Son
of Man standing on the right hand of God'.[1]

The question of the origin and meaning of the title is
still eagerly discussed[2] and cannot by any means be regarded as settled. Certain points, however, are reasonably
clear. Ὁ υἱὸς τοῦ ἀνθρώπου is a clumsy attempt to
translate the Aramaic *bar nasha*, 'man'. It has been
maintained that *bar nasha* cannot mean anything more
than 'a man' or 'man' in general;[3] but it is now widely
recognised that it can bear the sense of 'the Man', and so
could be used as a name for the Messiah; but whether it

---

[1] In the Apocalypse of John use is made of the phrase 'One like unto
a son of man' in descriptions of the Exalted Christ based on the imagery of
Dan. vii. 13. Cf. Apoc. i. 13, xiv. 14.

[2] See Jackson and Lake, *The Beginnings of Christianity*, i. 368ff.;
T. W. Manson, *The Teaching of Jesus*, 211f.; V. Taylor, *Jesus and His
Sacrifice*, 21-32; *ET*, lviii. 12-5; R. Otto, *The Kingdom of God and the Son
of Man*, 159-261; N. Messel, *Der Menschensohn in den Bilderreden des
Henoch* (1922); E. Sjöberg, *Der Menschensohn im Äthiopischen Henochbuch*
(1944); J. Y. Campbell, *JTS*, xlviii. 145-55; J. Bowman, *ET*, lix.
283-8; M. Black, *ET*, lx. 11-5, 32-6, 321f.

[3] By J. Wellhausen, *Skizzen und Vorarbeiten*, vi. 187-215 and H. Lietz-
mann, *Der Menschensohn* (1896).

was used in this sense in the days of Jesus is disputed.[1]
The idea has been traced back to Iranian thought, and,
in particular, to the ancient myth of Primal Man.[2]   The
later teaching concerning the Son of Man is rooted in the
Old Testament and is developed in the Apocalyptic
Literature.   In Ezekiel the phrase is used very frequently
by the prophet as a human self-designation.   'And he
said unto me, Son of Man, stand upon thy feet, and I will
speak with thee' (ii. 1), is the first of many examples of the
kind.   In Psa. viii. 4 it is used as a synonym for 'man' in
the well-known words:

> 'What is man, that thou art mindful of him?
> And the son of man, that thou visitest him,'

and again in Psa. lxxx. 17 (cf. 15) in the couplet:

> 'Let thy hand be upon the man of thy right hand,
> Upon the son of man whom thou madest strong for thyself'.

In Dan. vii. 13 the phrase 'one like unto a son of man'
describes a human figure who is brought to the Ancient
of Days, and represents the Jewish community, 'the saints
of the Most High', to whom are promised 'dominion, and
glory, and a kingdom' (vii. 14, 27).   In the Apocalyptic
Literature a marked development of this conception is
seen in the Similitudes of I Enoch (xxxvii-lxxi), where the
Son of Man is a superhuman being, 'the Elect One',
whose name is at present concealed, but who is destined
to be revealed as the Judge of men and the Messianic
Ruler in the Kingdom of God.   A similar idea appears
also in 4 Ezra xiii, in the vision of the Man rising from

---

[1] See Otto, op. cit., Sjöberg, op. cit., and the articles mentioned above of
J. Bowman and M. Black.

[2] Cf. the article of J. M. Creed, 'The Heavenly Man', *JTS*, xxvi,
113-36, also, for Babylonian parallels, C. Kraeling, *Anthropos and the Son
of Man* (1927), 145ff.

the Sea, who destroys a hostile multitude, and afterwards calls to himself 'another multitude which was peaceable' including some who were glad, some sorrowful, some in bonds, and some leading victims. There can be no doubt that in certain circles the Son of Man was conceived as a Superhuman Messiah, in contrast with the ruling conception of the human Son of David, but there is good reason, I believe, to think that Jesus's use of the title was independently derived from reflection upon the basic Old Testament passage, Dan. vii. 13.[1] The questions to be discussed are; What did He mean by the term, and How did He apply it to Himself?

The relevant sayings in the Gospels have often been examined. For our present purpose it will be enough to assemble these sayings noting those which are of doubtful authenticity, and classifying and examining the rest.

II

In Mk the title is found fourteen times, twice before the great day of Caesarea Philippi, when Jesus asked the disciples, 'Who say you that I am?' (viii. 29), and twelve times after this event. The two sayings, ii. 10 and ii. 28, which have a present significance, have frequently been set aside as being cases in which *bar nasha* was erroneously interpreted as a title in the primitive tradition, the true meaning being 'man'.[2] It is more probable, I believe, that ii. 10, 'The Son of Man hath authority upon earth to forgive sins', is a genuine utterance, which Jesus spoke without the expectation of being immediately understood,

---

[1] Cf. T. W. Manson, *op. cit.*, 229; V. Taylor, *op. cit.*, 27f.; C. J. Cadoux, *The Historic Mission of Jesus*, 99f.; W. Manson, *Jesus the Messiah*, 117, 120. But see Otto, *op. cit.*, 176ff.

[2] See the commentaries on Mk of Wellhausen, 16, Klostermann, 27, and Branscomb, 43f.; also T. W. Manson, *op. cit.*, 214, Jackson and Lake *op. cit.*, i. 375; Cadoux, *op. cit.*, 75, 96.

and that ii. 28, 'So that the Son of Man is lord even of the sabbath', is an early comment on the saying, 'The sabbath was made for man, and not man for the sabbath'.[1] Of the remaining twelve sayings nine[2] are Passion-sayings, which speak of the rejection and suffering of the Son of Man, who 'came to give his life a ransom for many' (x. 45), and three are eschatological, viii. 38, xiii. 26, xiv. 62. Of these three viii. 38 may be communal, and xiv. 62 voices the conviction that the priests will see fulfilled in Jesus the destiny described in Psa. cx. 1 and Dan. vii. 13.[3]

Apparently, Q contained eleven Son of Man sayings, most of which are available for our inquiry, after allowance has been made for the possibility that in some cases the original use of *bar nasha* has been misunderstood.[4] None of these sayings refers to Messianic suffering; four[5] appear to have a present significance; and six[6] are Parousia-sayings. Some of the sayings may have a communal reference, but in most cases the reference is to Jesus Himself.

Of the six sayings taken from the M source by Matthew two (xiii. 37 and 41) belong to the secondary interpretation of the Parable of the Tares, and four (x. 23, xix. 28, xxiv. 30, and xxv. 31) are Parousia-sayings. Of

---

[1] I have discussed ii. 10 and 28 in *The Gospel according to St. Mark*, 197-201, 219f.

[2] Mk. viii. 31, ix. 9, 12, 31, x. 33, 45, xiv. 21 (*bis*), 41.

[3] See *The Gospel according to St. Mark*, 568f.

[4] Possibly in Lk. vi. 22 = Mt. v. 11 ('for my sake') and less probably in I k. xii. 8f. = Mt. x. 32f. ('I'). The text of Lk. xvii. 22 (No parallel in Mt) is uncertain; cf. Dodd, *The Parables of the Kingdom*, 108*n*; Torrey, *The Four Gospels*, 312; T. W. Manson, *The Sayings of Jesus*, 142.

[5] Lk. vi. 22 = Mt. v. 11, Lk. vii. 24 = Mt. xi. 19, Lk. ix. 58 = Mt. viii. 20, Lk. xi. 30 = Mt. xii. 40.

[6] Lk. xii. 8f. = Mt. x. 32f., Lk. xii. 10 = Mt. xii. 32, Lk. xii. 40 = Mt. xxiv. 44, Lk. xvii. 24 = Mt. xxiv. 27, Lk. xvii. 26 = Mt. xxiv. 37, Lk. xvii. 30 (No parallel in Mt).

these four sayings Mt. x. 23, 'You will not have gone
through the cities of Israel, till the Son of Man be come',
has long rested under critical suspicion on the ground
that 'it reflects the experience and the expectations of the
primitive Palestinian Church'.[1] I doubt, however,
whether the saying should be regarded as inadmissible
for the meaning of the title 'Son of Man'.[2] It may well
have been *re-interpreted* by Matthew in the light of the
controversy regarding the Gentile Mission; but it is
difficult to think that is was *invented* for this purpose. It
is possible, indeed, that in rejecting it we may be destroy-
ing evidence, for it is a plain simple statement in marked
contrast with xiii. 41, xix. 28, xxiv. 30, and xxv. 31.
These passages are the most highly coloured of the
Parousia-sayings, and, since Matthew has undoubtedly
embellished Mk. viii. 38 (cf. Mt. xvi. 27) and Mk. xiii.
27 (cf. Mt. xxiv. 31) with Apocalyptic imagery, there is
every reason to think that the same is true of the
M-sayings.

The L source, used by Luke, probably contained seven
Son of Man sayings. Of these xvii. 25, xix. 10, xxii. 48,
and xxiv. 7 are Passion-sayings, the last being a post-
Resurrection saying. They support the evidence of Mk,
but add no new element, except that xvii. 25 implies that
the Parousia is subsequent to the suffering of the Son of
Man. The remaining three sayings are eschatological.
Unlike Mk. xiv. 62, Lk. xxii. 69 speaks only of the
session of the Son of Man at the right hand of the power of
God. Lk. xviii. 8b and Lk. xxi. 36 both refer to the

---

[1] So T. W. Manson, *The Sayings of Jesus*, 182. Cf. also V. H.
Stanton, *The Gospels as Historical Documents*, ii. 330; B. H. Streeter, *The
Four Gospels*, 255, *The Primitive Church*, 34f.; C. J. Cadoux, *op. cit.*, 95.
Probably the saying has suffered in critical estimation from the use made of
it by Schweitzer in *The Quest of the Historical Jesus*, 264, 333, 357-9.

[2] Especially if its original meaning was communal.

Parousia, but do not use the imagery of Dan. vii. 13.

In addition to the sayings from the four principal Gospel sources mentioned already there are three into which Matthew himself has introduced the title, Mt. xvi. 13, 28, and xxvi. 2. A fourth possible example is Mt. xxiv. 39, which may, however, have been taken from Q or M. If we neglect these editorial passages, and the parallels to sayings already cited, there are at least 37 Son of Man sayings in the Synoptic Gospels derived from Q, Mk, M, and L. When every allowance has been made for errors of translation from the original Aramaic versions, there remains an impressive body of evidence that Jesus did speak frequently of the Son of Man, and in many, and perhaps in most, cases with reference to Himself. No title applied to him in these Gospels is so widely and so richly attested. There are also thirteen[1] references in Jn. Six of these sayings describe the divine Christ in His present human manifestation (i. 51, ix. 35) or His exaltation (iii. 13, v. 27, vi. 27, 62), and seven are Passion-sayings (iii. 14, vi. 53, viii. 28, xii. 23, 34a, 34b, xiii. 31) although there is no reference to suffering, but rather to glorifying. Thus, while the sayings reflect the Johannine idiom and are doctrinal, they represent a further development of Synoptic teaching.

What Jesus meant by the title, and how He came to use it in different senses, are more difficult questions; and to these we must now turn. The question is complicated by the probability that the title is used both as a communal and a personal term, and by the fact that the sayings fall into three classes, according as the reference is to the present, to the future, and to Messianic suffering.

[1] If 'Son of Man' is read in ix. 35. Cf. the Commentaries of Bernard, 338 and Hoskyns, 414.

III

Since T. W. Manson wrote his *Teaching of Jesus* (1931)
much interest has been taken in the communal interpretation of the Son of Man.   Similar views have been endorsed by C. J. Cadoux[1] and other writers,[2] and independently the communal interpretation of the Son of
Man in 1 Enoch was put forward by Nils Messel in 1922.
This hypothesis does not rule out the view that the title
was also used by Jesus as a personal designation.   Manson's
submission is that the prophetic mission of Jesus is 'to
create the Son of Man, the Kingdom of the saints of the
Most High.'   In words often quoted he says: 'Finally,
when it becomes apparent that not even the disciples are
ready to rise to the demands of the ideal, he stands alone,
embodying in his own person the perfect human response
to the regal claims of God.'[3]

The communal interpretation of 1 Enoch is, I think
doubtful;[4] but it is relevant in some of the sayings in the
Gospels.   In this matter commentators can only record
their opinions, recognizing that it is only as these are
endorsed or rejected that progress is made.   With this
proviso I suggest that the Son of Man is the Elect
Community in the original form of the saying on being
ashamed of Jesus in Mk. viii. 38, and in allied Q sayings
on confessing and denying Him in Lk. xii. 8f. = Mt. x.
32f.   It may well be that some of the eschatological sayings were originally communal, in particular, Mt. x. 23,

[1] *The Historic Mission of Jesus*, 90-103.
[2] Cf. M. Black, *ET*, lx, 33f., 'In the passages discussed by Dr. Manson,
the communal meaning is not only possible, but highly probable, and may
be the true one, but it is doubtful if, in any case, it is the only one, and
nothing short of unambiguous evidence is required to demonstrate the
point.'
[3] *Op. cit.*, 228.
[4] I have discussed this view in *Jesus and His Sacrifice*, 24f.

Lk. xii. 40, xvii. 22, 24, 26, 30. The Passion-sayings are
personal, but a communal reference cannot be dismissed
in Lk. xvii. 25 and Mk. viii. 31, since elsewhere Jesus
declared that His intimate disciples were to share His cup
(Mk. x. 39; cf. viii. 34, xiv. 33), and because 'communal'
and 'personal' are not mutually exclusive categories.
Certainly there are many sayings in which the personal
aspect is unmistakable, as, for example, Mk. ii. 10,
ix. 9, 31, x. 33f., 45, xiv. 21, 41, and Lk. vii. 34, ix. 58,
xi. 30, xviii. 8*b*, xix. 10, xxii. 48. By the Son of Man
Jesus meant Himself, but sometimes the Elect Community
of which He is the Head.

How are we to relate the three groups of sayings already
distinguished, those which have a present significance,
those which point to the future, and those which speak of
suffering and rising again? The simplest expedient is to
eliminate two of these groups as Bultmann[1] does, by
attributing the first to mistranslation and the third to the
work of the Hellenistic Christian community. But these
are proposals to cut the knot. Mistranslation has frequently been suggested, with ill success in the case of
Mk. ii. 10, and with no better reason in Lk. vii. 34, ix. 58,
and xii. 10; and to assign the Passion-sayings to the
community is a suggestion far less convincing than the
view that Jesus Himself creatively re-interpreted the idea
of the Son of Man in terms of the Servant conception.
The three groups must stand. The greater difficulty is
the sharpness with which the Passion-sayings stand apart
from the Parousia-sayings, and the problem of associ-
ating the two series.[2] Why does Jesus speak in the third
person of the coming of the Son of Man *after* He has said

[1] *Theologie des Neuen Testaments*, 31. Of the Passion-sayings he asks,
Aber kann ein Zweifel daran sein, dass sie alle *vaticinia ex eventu* sind?
[2] *Op. cit.*, 30.

that, as the Son of Man, He must suffer? He does not speak of a *second* coming, a term which is not used in Christian literature until the middle of the second century.[1] The only way of meeting this difficulty adequately is the bold hypothesis that there was a development in the thought of Jesus during the course of His ministry, and that historically the Parousia-sayings came first.

Hitherto we have been prevented from taking this step by the fact that in the Gospels the Parousia-sayings stand last. There is good reason, however, to think that this arrangement is artificial, being occasioned by the strong Advent Hope of primitive Christianity. In an article in *The Expository Times*[2] I have attempted to show that almost all the Parousia-sayings appear either in the artificially compiled Apocalyptic Discourses of Mk. xiii, Lk. xvii, and xxi, or as isolated sayings; and from the evidence I suggested that 'with the exception of Mk. xiv. 62 and Mt. x. 23, no "Son of Man" saying relative to the Parousia need be assigned to the last stages of the Ministry, but may equally well belong to any stage, even the earliest'.[3]

If this opinion is sound, we are at liberty to undertake the task of historical reconstruction, even if the results are provisional and perhaps speculative. The construction to which we are led is as follows. Jesus began His ministry with the announcement of the imminence of the Kingdom of God and the coming of the Son of Man. At this period the prophecies are eschatological. They are susceptible of being interpreted either of a supernatural

---

[1] Bultmann cites Justin Martyr, *Dial.*, *xiv*. 8, xl. 4, cxviii. 2.

[2] *ET*, lviii. 12-15. 'The Apocalyptic Document embedded in Mk. xiii is a lodestone which has attracted to itself the majority of the sayings about the coming of the Son of Man', *op. cit.*, 13. Cf. Lk. xvii and xxi.

[3] *Op. cit.*, 13.

person other than Himself, or of the Elect Community
of the Son of Man, the latter being the more probable in
view of the use Jesus makes of Dan. vii rather than
1 Enoch. The climax of this period is where Schweitzer
placed it, the Mission of the Twelve (Mk. vi. 6*b*-13).
Probably already Jesus had applied the term 'Son of Man'
to Himself, but whether this is so or not, this usage is
characteristic of the early ministry in several of the sayings
with a present and personal significance. As the Son of
Man, He has authority on earth to forgive sins (Mk. ii. 10).
Unlike the Baptist, He had come eating and drinking,
and men said of Him that He was a gluttonous man and a
winebibber, a friend of taxgatherers and sinners (Lk. vii.
34). Son of Man, though He was, He had nowhere to
lay His head (Lk. ix. 58). As Jonah became a sign to the
Ninevites, so He would be on His generation (Lk. xi. 30).
After the failure of the Mission, and the withdrawal to
'the region of Tyre' (Mk. vii. 24ff.), He emerges near
Caesarea Philippi, and teaches His disciples that the Son
of Man 'must suffer' (Mk. viii. 31), and after repeated and
vain attempts to impart this teaching, consummates His
ministry by His rejection, dying, and rising again. In
such a historical reconstruction it is not necessary to think
of one representation of the doctrine of the Son of Man as
first presented, then rejected, and finally replaced by
others. The process is one of unfolding and enlargement
rather than successive substitution. All the interpretations of the Son of Man meet us in the declaration to the
priests (Mk. xiv. 62) that they would see the prophecies
of Psa. cx. 1 and Dan. vii. 13 fulfilled, and the Advent
Hope itself is more surely based in the necessary idea of a
final consummation rather than on the Parousia-sayings of
the eschatological discourses which themselves refer to the
first coming of the Son of Man. The details of such

constructions must necessarily be speculative, and they are mentioned here primarily to show that the different groups of sayings are fully credible in the Story of Jesus.

For our present inquiry the importance of the title is its meaning for the person of Jesus. It is the name chosen by Him, in conscious preference, we must suppose, to the more colourless 'Christos' and the human and nationalistic title 'Son of David'. It expresses the idea of lordship, of rule over the Messianic community, and its associations are supernatural. Strange to the Gentile world, it embodies His conception of Messiahship, as the more familiar names could not do, and perhaps in particular the idea of a concealed Messiahship yet to be manifested in action. Whether in this respect, it is influenced by 1 Enoch xlviii. 2, 3, 6 we cannot tell, but undoubtedly there is a certain similarity in the idea of the Son of Man named in the presence of the Lord of Spirits, chosen and hidden before the creation of the world and for evermore. And this we must believe to be the idea of Jesus Himself, if we reject, as we are compelled to reject, Wrede's hypothesis that the 'Messianic Secret' is a literary device of Mark. And yet, even so the Son of Man concept is not wide and rich enough to express what Jesus believes concerning His person and work. That is why He reinterprets the idea in terms of the Suffering Servant, teaches that the Son of Man must suffer, and in this persuasion goes deliberately to Jerusalem to die, convinced that He is fulfilling the purpose of His Father, with which He has completely identified Himself.

VIII
THE SERVANT

IT will be convenient next to consider the title Servant, even though it is not used by Jesus, and is found in the New Testament only in Ac. iii. 13, 26, iv. 27, 30.[1] Nevertheless, the influence of the Servant-conception, as distinct from the use of the title, is far-reaching. It is seen in the words of the divine voice in Mk. i. 11, 'Thou art my beloved Son; with thee I am well pleased', in the Passion-sayings of Mk. viii. 31, ix. 31, x. 33f., 45; in the saying, Lk. xxii. 37, 'For I say unto you, that this which is written must be fulfilled in me, And he was reckoned with transgressors'; in Matthew's application of Isa. liii. 4 to the healing ministry in the words, 'Himself took our infirmities, and bare our diseases' (Mt. viii. 17), and of Isa. xlii. 1-4 in Mt. xii. 18-21; and as one of the elements which have influenced the saying in Jn. i. 29, 'Behold, the Lamb of God, which taketh away the sin of the world!'. Outside the Gospels its influence is manifest in Rom. iv. 25 and Phil. ii. 5-11, and possibly in 1 Cor. xv. 3f.; in Heb. ix. 28, and in 1 Pet. ii. 22-5; and in the Apostolic Fathers, in 1 Clem. xvi, Barn. v. 2, and in the Didache, ix. 2f., x. 2f. In view of the popularity of the Servant-conception in primitive Christianity, and its place in liturgical usage, in prayers (Ac. iv. 27, 30, Did. ix. 2f., x. 2f.) and in hymns (Phil. ii. 5-11), in early confessions (1 Cor. xv. 3f.) and in exhortations (1 Clem.

[1] In the Jerusalem A source, as described by Harnack, *The Acts of the Apostles*, Eng. tr., 162-202, 241-5, and Jackson and Lake, *The Beginnings of Christianity*, ii. 126-57.

xvi), it is a mark of the fidelity of the Evangelists to historic tradition that it emerges so rarely in the Gospels, and with manifest restraint in the sayings of Jesus. In the circumstances one cannot fail to be conscious of a healthy scepticism concerning the alleged activity of Hellenistic Christianity in the formation of the Servant-tradition. In the usage of Jesus the influence of the Servant-conception is adjectival; it is the undertone of His teaching concerning Messianic suffering. The title 'Son of Man' is not abandoned in favour of 'the Servant'. On the contrary, it continues to be used exclusively, but with a richer and a deeper meaning. It is as if a familiar air were developed and transposed into a minor key, suggestive of pain and tragedy, in which the royal and kingly note of the original phrase is not lost, but transformed.

IX

THE LORD

WHILE Jesus spoke of Himself as 'the Son of Man', the earliest Christian community, after the Resurrection, expressed its veneration for Him, as the Risen and Ascended Lord, by the use of the term 'the Lord'. Many factors played their part in establishing the use of this title, especially those of worship and of personal devotion to the Living Christ. Since Wilhelm Bousset published his stimulating book, *Kyrios Christos*,[1] now some forty years ago, the question has been eagerly debated whether the use of the title arose spontaneously in the primitive communities, or whether it was carried over from the Hellenistic world with its religious associations and applied to Jesus by the first Christians. The Christological importance of this problem is obvious, but its interest is far more than apologetic; it raises the question of the estimate the believing community held concerning Jesus, and the grounds on which it rested. It is necessary first to consider the meaning and associations of the title, and then the manner and extent of its use in the New Testament, since it is upon these points that the significance of its application to Jesus depends.

I

The word κύριος means 'owner', 'master', 'lord', and

[1] 1913, 3rd ed., 1926. To the criticisms of P. Wernle, *ZThK.* xxv· (1915) Bousset replied in *Jesus der Herr* (1916). Cf. also W. Foerster *Herr ist Jesus* (1924), *KThW.*, iii. 1038-56, 1081-94; E. Lohmeyer *Kyrios Jesus* (1928). See the important discussion of A. E. J. Rawlinson *The NT. Doctrine of the Christ* (1926), 39f., 92-107, 231-7.

it is used in this sense in the parables of Jesus.[1] It is also used in the Gospels by a son of his father (Mt. xxi. 30) and in addressing a superior with courtesy and respect (Mt. xxvii. 63, Ac. xvi. 30, etc.). In the Septuagint the word is commonly employed to render the Hebrew *Adonai*, 'Lord', and, what is more important, it is the usual substitute for the personal name 'Yahweh'. It is not limited, however, to this religious usage, being freely employed as a term of honour for angels and men (cf. Gen. xix. 2, xxvii. 29, 32, etc.). As applied to God, with or without the definite article, it denotes His power over the world and men, as the Creator, the Ruler, and the giver of life and death.[2] In the Greek world it was widely used as a cult-name, in Caesar-worship and in the Mystery-religions.[3] In an inscription dated 62 B.C. it is used in Egypt of Ptolemy XIII, who is described as 'the lord, king, God'. It was also used of Herod the Great and of Agrippa I and II, and increasingly it was applied to the Roman Emperors, Caligula, Claudius, Nero, and Domitian, the latter being described as *Dominus et deus noster*. Deissmann observes that 'everywhere, down to the remotest village, the officials called Nero *Kyrios*'.[4] In the Mystery-religions it was applied to Osiris, Sarapis, and Hermes-Thoth, and κύρια is used of Isis, Artemis of Ephesus, and the Great Mother, Cybele. Of many examples the best known are P. Fay, 127 (ii/iii. A.D.), '. . . I supplicate the Lord Sarapis on your behalf', and P. Oxy. I, 110 (ii/A.D.), 'Chaeremon requests your com-

---

[1] Cf. Mk. xii. 9, 'What therefore will the lord of the vineyard do?'; Mt. xviii. 25, 'His lord commanded him to be sold'; Mt. xxv. 20, 'Lord, you delivered unto me five talents'; Lk. xiii. 8, etc.

[2] Cf. G. Quell, *KThW*. iii. 1056-80.

[3] Cf. A. Deissmann, *Light from the Ancient East*, 349-62; W. Bousset, *Kryios Christos*, 91-101; W. Foerster, *KThW.*, iii. 1048-56.

[4] *Op. cit.*, 353.

D

pany at dinner at the table of the Lord Sarapis in the
Serapaeum to-morrow, the 15th, at 9 o'clock'.[1]   It is
therefore with justice that Deissmann writes, 'It may be
said with certainty that at the time when Christianity
originated "Lord" was a divine predicate intelligible to the
whole Eastern world'.[2]

It is certainly a possible hypothesis that the name
Kyrios, with its religious associations, was borrowed from
Greek religion and applied to Jesus.   Bousset reminds us
that it was in the atmosphere of the Kyrios-cult that the
Greek speaking community at Antioch in Syria came into
being and grew to maturity.   In this milieu, he claims,
the young Christian religion was formed as a Christ-cult,
and from this environment κύριος was taken over to
describe the dominating place of Jesus in public worship.[3]   The process completed itself unconsciously in
the uncontrollable depth of the soul of a community
which surrendered itself to the prevailing atmosphere.
It was in the nature of things that the first Hellenistic
Christian communities gave to their Cult-Hero the title
κύριος.[4]

It remains to be considered whether this explanation is
an adequate hypothesis, and whether other factors connected with the earliest Christian tradition need to be
taken more fully into account, especially 'the dominating
place of Jesus in public worship'.   Here, however, it may
be said, that, even if 'the prevailing atmosphere' facili-
tated the use of the title, we have still to explain how it
came to be applied to Jesus.   A simple process of borrowing can never be a sufficient explanation even if it took
place in 'the uncontrollable depth of the soul of a
community'.

---

[1] Cf. Moulton and Milligan, *VGT.*, 365.   [2] *Op. cit.*, 350.
[3] *Op. cit.*, 99.   [4] *Ibid.*

II

It is necessary next to examine the use of the term 'Lord' as it is applied to Jesus in the Gospels, the Acts, and the Epistles.

We may simplify our task by leaving almost out of account the cases in which the vocative κύριε is applied to Jesus in the Gospels,[1] since its Hebrew equivalent, 'Rabbi', is used in like manner when pupils address their master.[2] F. C. Burkitt suggests that in the Synoptic Gospels the nearest equivalent to κύριε is 'Milord', and the Fourth Gospel 'Sir'.[3] The vocative, of course, can express all ranges of feeling, from simple respect to reverential awe; it carries what it is made to bear. And it is hardly to be doubted that in some cases, when κύριε is addressed to Jesus, it is more than an expression of courtesy. In these matters, however, we cannot get beyond impression and suppositions. Moreover, its use is often editorial.[4] To some extent the same is true of ὁ κύριος, but here the situation is more definite and the connotation of the word is richer.

The usage of the Gospels suggests that ὁ κύριος was not used of Jesus during His ministry, but was applied to Him subsequently to His Resurrection, although with what interval we cannot determine. It is not found in Q, and there is only a single example in Mk and Mt, in the message of Jesus with reference to the colt, 'The Lord hath need of him' (Mk. xi. 3 = Mt. xxi. 3 = Lk. xix. 31, 34). Here the phrase is commonly held to mean 'The

---

[1] The only example in Mk is vii. 28, unless it is read in i. 40 and x. 51. In Mt it is found about 20 times; cf. Lk (17) and Jn (30). For Q see Lk. vi. 46, vii. 6.

[2] Cf. Foerster, *KThW.*, iii. 1083f.

[3] *Christian Beginnings*, 46.

[4] Cf. Mk. iv. 38, Mt. viii. 25, and Lk. viii. 24.

Master',[1] but I prefer to think that it is a reference to the owner of the colt, and it seems to me a dubious inference that the Evangelist is drawing upon a tradition to the effect that in certain circles Jesus was already spoken of as 'the Lord' during His lifetime.[2] Far more important is a second passage in Mk, in which Jesus refers to the fact that in Psa. cx. 1 the Messiah is described as κύριος, and says, 'David calleth him Lord; and whence is he his son?' (Mk. xii. 37 = Mt. xxii. 45 = Lk. xx. 44). This use of Psa. cx. 1 by Jesus[3] may be one of the factors in the application to Him of the name 'the Lord' by the first Christians.

In the Gospels the first extensive use of ὁ κύριος begins with Luke. In addition to xix. 31, 34, which repeat Mk. xi. 3, the title is used fifteen times in narratives derived from Q and L,[4] and twice in the Birth Stories of Lk. i, ii.[5] In most of the narratives it appears in the phrase 'And the Lord said', or its equivalent, and in no case is there any question of primitive usage; the name belongs to terminology of the Caesarean community. The same is true of the Lukan Birth Stories. Only in Lk. xxiv. 34 does it appear in a saying, in the post-Resurrection message, 'The Lord is risen indeed'. The usage is like that of the spurious ending of Mk, in xvi. 19, 'So then the Lord Jesus, after he had spoken unto them,

---

[1] See the commentaries of Swete, 248, Rawlinson, 152, and Lagrange, 289.

[2] *The Gospel according to St. Mark*, 455.

[3] It is unsatisfactory to assign Mk. xii. 35-7 to the Christian community, as Bousset, 43, does. Christians who held Jesus to be of the seed of David (Rom. i. 3) were not likely to attribute to Him the question, 'Whence is he his son?'.

[4] Lk. vii. 13, 19, x. 1, 39, 41, xi. 39, xii. 42, xiii. 15, xvii. 5, 6, xviii. 6, xix. 8, xxii. 61 (*bis*), xxiv. 34. In some MSS the title also appears in xxii. 31 and xxiv. 3.

[5] Lk. i. 43, 'the mother of my Lord', and ii. 11, 'a Saviour, which is Christ, the Lord'.

was received up into heaven', and in xvi. 20, 'And they went forth, and preached everywhere, the Lord working with them, and confirming the word by the signs which followed'.

The Fourth Gospel supplies an impressive confirmation of the view that ὁ κύριος is a post-Resurrection title. In Jn. i-xix., in the commonly accepted text, there are three examples of the use of the name in iv. 1, vi. 23, and xi. 2, but in each case, on textual and exegetical grounds, there is good reason to think that ὁ κύριος is a copyist's gloss.[1] Also in the saying in xiii. 32f., in which the title appears twice, ὁ κύριος is used as a 'titular nominative', implying the use of κύριε mentioned above.[2] In contrast, in xx. and xxi., there are nine examples of ὁ κύριος, three in Resurrection narratives[3] and six in post-Resurrection sayings.[4] It is clear that the Evangelist feels it appropriate to speak of 'the Lord' in these contexts, but does not feel at liberty to use the title in connexion with the earlier ministry.

From this evidence we must conclude that it is highly improbable that this title was in use in the lifetime of Jesus. It is as the Risen and Ascended Lord that He is ὁ κύριος.

How freely the title was used in primitive Christianity appears in the Acts of the Apostles. Here, as in the Epistles, it is used, in combination with other names, in the names, 'the Lord Jesus',[5] 'the Lord Jesus Christ',[6]

---

[1] Cf. J. H. Bernard, *St. John*, 132, 189, 372, and for iv. 1 and vi. 23, Hoskyns, *The Fourth Gospel*, 252, 328.

[2] Cf. Bernard, *op. cit.*, 465.

[3] Jn. xx. 20, xxi. 7*b*, 12.

[4] Jn. xx. 2, 13, 18, 25, 28, xxi. 7*a*.

[5] Ac. i. 21, iv. 33, viii. 16, xi. 20, xv. 11, xvi. 31, xix. 5, 13, 17, xx. 24, 35, xxi. 13, xxviii. 31.

[6] Ac. xi. 17.

and 'Our Lord Jesus Christ',[1] but more frequent and distinctive is the use of the name 'the Lord'. Sir John C. Hawkins has computed that the latter is used in narrative perhaps twenty times.[2] But if we add editorial passages, it is used twenty-six times,[3] even when we have left out of account passages in which the phrase is probably used of God.[4] In ii. 36 κύριος and Χριστός are combined in the impassioned exhortation, 'Let all the house of Israel therefore know assuredly, that God hath made him both Lord and Christ, this Jesus whom you crucified', and in x. 36 he is declared to be 'Lord of all'.[5] Although the date of the Acts is late, this use of the title probably represents the earliest preaching with fidelity, and it is significant that the great majority of the passages are found in the first half of the book.

The evidence of the Pauline Epistles is decisive. Hawkins points out that in the New Testament Epistles ὁ κύριος is found perhaps forty-six times;[6] but, if we limit ourselves to St. Paul, and extend the enumeration beyond cases in which it is used of the Risen and Ascended Christ, including phrases in which the article is naturally omitted, as, for example, the phrase ἐν κυρίῳ, we find at least one hundred and thirty passages in which St. Paul speaks of the Lord,[7] in addition to those in which he uses the names 'Our Lord', 'our Lord Jesus Christ', 'the Lord

---

[1] Ac. xv. 26, xx. 21.

[2] Horae Synopticae, 43.

[3] Ac. ii. 36, v. 14, ix. 1, 10, 11, 15, 17, 27, 28, 35, 42, x. 33, 36, xi. 16, 23, 24, xiii. 12, 49, xiv. 3, 23, xv. 35, 36, 40, xviii. 8, 9, 25.

[4] Ac. ii. 47, iii. 20, viii. 22, 24, 25, ix. 31, xi. 21, xii. 17, 24, xiii. 2, 47, 48, xvi. 14, 15.

[5] In these two passages the article is omitted because in ii. 36 κύριος is used predicatively and in x. 36 is defined by the gen. πάντων.

[6] Op. cit., 43.

[7] Rom (16 times), 1 Cor (44), 2 Cor (17), Gal (2), Eph (16), Phil (10), Col (10), 1 Thess (11), 2 Thess (7), Philm (2).

Jesus Christ', and many other kindred expressions.[1] This evidence points, not only to St. Paul's usage, but to that of Gentile Christianity at large, for which Jesus is pre-eminently 'the Lord'. No other name of Jesus is used with anything like the same frequency. 'The Lord' is at once the historical Jesus, whose commands bind believers (1 Cor. vii. 10, 12, 25, ix. 14), and the Exalted Christ, who invests His servants with authority (2 Cor. x. 8, xiii. 10) and receives their service (Rom. xii. 11, Eph. vi. 7). He is the Coming One (1 Thess. iv. 16, v. 2, 1 Cor. v. 5), the Judge (1 Thess. iv. 6, 1 Cor. iv. 4f.), the ruler over the living and the dead (Rom. xiv. 9), the Lord of all men (Rom. x. 12), the One Lord (Eph. iv. 5), the dispenser, with the Father, of grace and peace (Rom. i. 7, 1 Cor. i. 3, etc.), the One in whose name every knee shall bow, and every tongue confess His lordship (Phil. ii. 11). Nor does St. Paul stand alone. The same terminology in various forms appears in the Pastoral[2] and Catholic Epistles,[3] and in the Apocalypse of John[4] where Christ is hymned as 'king of kings and lord of lords' (xxii. 14, xix. 16).

The New Testament evidence shows how early the use of the title ὁ κύριος arose, and how deeply it is connected

---

[1] 'Our Lord' (1), 'Our Lord Jesus Christ' (28), 'The Lord Jesus Christ' (18), 'Jesus Christ our Lord' (3), 'Christ Jesus our Lord' (6, including 'my Lord' and 'the Lord'), 'Jesus our Lord' (2), 'Our Lord Christ' (1), 'Our Lord Jesus' (9), 'The Lord Jesus' (12), 'The Lord Christ' (1), 'One Lord, Jesus Christ' (1). In all such lists textual variants leave a small measure of uncertainty.

[2] Pastoral Epistles: 'The Lord' (12 times), 'Our Lord' (2), 'Our Lord Jesus Christ' (2), 'Christ Jesus our Lord' (2).

[3] Catholic Epistles: 'The Lord' (10), 'Our Lord Jesus Christ' (10), 'The Lord Jesus Christ' (2), 'Jesus Christ our Lord' (1), 'Jesus our Lord' (1). In 2 Pet 'and Saviour' is added five times.

[4] Apocalypse: 'The Lord' (4), 'The Lord Jesus' (1). Cf. Hebrews: 'The Lord' (2), 'Our Lord' (1), 'Our Lord Jesus' (1). There are no examples in Titus or in the Johannine Epistles.

with the worship of the primitive Christian Church. In the earliest letters of St. Paul the terminology, and the ideas associated with it, are freely used and with no suggestion of being an innovation. As Bousset shows, the conception of Jesus as Lord was not the special work of St. Paul, but, on the contrary, one which already existed in Christian communities at Antioch, Damascus, and Tarsus.[1] In primitive Christian piety, he maintains, the correlative to the title 'the Lord Christ' was not the individual, but 'the community, the ἐκκλησία, the σῶμα τοῦ Χριστοῦ', and the community as organized for worship.[2] Many considerations favour this view. When St. Paul speaks of confessing with the mouth 'Jesus as Lord' (Rom. x. 9), he implies the existence of a primitive Christian creed 'Jesus is Lord', and so too when he writes, 'No man can say, Jesus is Lord, but in the Holy Spirit' (1 Cor. xii. 3).[3] 'We preach not ourselves', he says, 'but Christ Jesus as Lord' (2 Cor. iv. 5). When he describes Christians as 'those who call upon the name of our Lord Jesus Christ' (1 Cor. i. 2; cf. Ac. ix. 14, 21, xxii. 16, 2 Tim. ii. 22)—a formula which, significantly enough, goes back to Joel ii. 32—he is alluding to invocations of Christ, in confessions, hymns, and ejaculations in Christian worship, and to prayers and thanksgivings to God 'in his name' (cf. 1 Cor. i. 20, Eph. v. 20, etc.). Again, the idea of the Lord of believers is closely connected with the most central acts of the cultus. When St. Paul reminds the Corinthians that they 'were washed', 'sanctified', and 'justified', he is thinking of Baptism, and he connects it with 'the name of our Lord Jesus Christ' and 'the Spirit of our God' (1 Cor. vi. 11). He describes the Eucharist

[1] *Op. cit.*, 90. Cf. Bultmann, *Theologie des Neuen Testaments*, 124.
[2] Bousset, *op. cit.*, 90.
[3] Cf. O. Cullmann, *The Earliest Christian Confessions*, 41, 55-62.

as 'the Lord's supper' (κυριακὸν δεῖπνον) in 1 Cor. xi. 20, and contrasts 'the table of the Lord' (τράπεζα κυρίου) with 'the table of daemons' (1 Cor. x. 21). Naturally this evidence comes from the life and practice of Gentile communities, but there is no ground, as we shall see, for connecting the worship of Jesus as Lord exclusively with the life of Hellenistic communities, as distinct from those that were Jewish-Christian. Indeed, the use of the invocation *Marana tha* 'Our Lord, come' (1 Cor. xvi. 22), which corresponds to the Greek phrase, 'Αμήν, ἔρχου κύριε Ἰησοῦ, 'Amen, come Lord Jesus', in Apoc. xxii. 20, shows unmistakably that the title 'Our Lord' was in familiar use in Aramaic speaking communities.

The fact that the title ὁ κύριος is so freely used in the Thessalonian Epistles, written in A.D. 51, implies that it had long been in use in early Christianity, at least in the decade A.D. 40-50, and probably much earlier. Liturgical usages do not grow up in a night, and we may justly infer that in Jewish-Christian circles they point back to the decade A.D. 30-40. The cry, 'The Lord is risen', contains at the most a negligible anachronism, and it is by no means excluded that historically it is the earliest use of the name.

III

We are now in a position to discuss the origin of the title 'the Lord' as it is applied to Jesus.

We may say at once that the hypothesis that it is derived, together with the ideas associated with it, from Hellenistic religious usage as illustrated in the Mystery-religions, is unsatisfactory. Several reasons support this claim.

First, the hypothesis assumes that St. Paul's usage, and indeed his theology as a whole, are predominantly Greek,

whereas there is every reason to believe, as Professor
W. D. Davies[1] has maintained, that his deepest affiliations
are Jewish. The passage, 1 Cor. viii. 5f., to which
reference is frequently made in support of the theory of
borrowing, tells in the opposite direction, for it is difficult
not to hear a note of scorn and conscious superiority in
the words: 'For though there be that are called gods,
whether in heaven or on earth, as there are gods many, and
lords many; yet to us there is one God, the Father, of
whom are all things, and we unto him; and one Lord, Jesus
Christ, through whom are all things, and we through him'.

Secondly, the hypothesis requires us to recognise a
cleft, one may say, a gulf, between the Christological
beliefs of the Hellenistic and Jewish-Christian communities, which has left no trace in the Acts of the Apostles or
any of the New Testament writings. The first Christians
differed in their views on circumcision and table-fellow-
ship with Gentiles, and, above all, on the Gentile Mission,
but we are devoid of evidence that there was any dispute
on the question whether Jesus was Lord.

Thirdly, the hypothesis suffers shipwreck on the fact
that Aramaic Christianity confessed Jesus as Lord.
A. E. J. Rawlinson[2] has justly observed that 'the phrase
Marana tha is in fact the Achilles' heel of the theory of
Bousset', who, after suggesting that the Aramaic-speaking
Christians of Antioch adopted the title in imitation of their
Greek-speaking brethren and rendered ὁ κύριος into
Aramaic as *Maran*, explained the formula in *Jesus der
Herr* as a Jewish curse, meaning 'Our Lord (i.e. God) will
come and judge you', and finally returned to his original
suggestion in the second edition of *Kyrios Christos* as 'a
possibility which cannot be ignored' and which 'must be

---

[1] *Paul and Rabbinic Judaism* (1949).
[2] *The New Testament Doctrine of the Christ*, 235.

taken seriously'. In these suggestions one hears the embarrassed advocate.

Lastly, the hypothesis in question is superficial. It is not a matter simply of the borrowing of a title, but of the ideas associated with it, and it is improbable that the name would have been applied to Jesus unless already He had been recognized as the object of veneration in personal experience and in worship. If this claim is admitted, the borrowing would be a mere matter of terminology, and further would be unnecessary if there was any reason in Christian teaching and belief to apply the name to Jesus. We must look much deeper if we are to account for the Christian use of the title.

It is not likely that the origin of the title is to be found in any single consideration. Several factors appear to have played their part.

Of these undoubtedly the most important is the Resurrection. How profoundly the Resurrection called for a richer apprehension of the person of Christ is illustrated in the classic passage in Rom. i. 4, 'declared to be the Son of God with power, according to the spirit of holiness, by the resurrection of the dead'. As we have seen, it is to the Resurrection that Wrede traced the Christian confession of Jesus as the Messiah. This explanation is much more credibly given to the recognition of Him as Lord, for the Resurrection revealed Him as the vanquisher of death and as the Living Christ who rightly claimed the absolute obedience of believers. It was no longer adequate to think of Him only as 'the Christ', still less as 'the Teacher' or 'the Prophet', while His own chosen name, 'the Son of Man', was too mysterious to become a generally used title. The Resurrection had given to His person a new dimension, and it was inevitable that He who must manifestly exercise lordship over

His community should be called 'the Lord'. This
necessity was deepened by the sense of His presence in
the earliest Christian assemblies, when the community
assembled in fellowship for the praise and worship of God
and met in daily expectation of the Parousia of Christ;
and most of all in 'the breaking of bread' as the Last
Supper was remembered and celebrated. Teaching
within the community must also have contributed to the
same end. It may be that it was remembered that in His
parables He had spoken of 'the lord of the vineyard'
(Mk. xii. 9) and as 'the Lord' of the servants to whom
talents were given (Mt. xxv. 19) and of the waiting
servants (Lk. xii. 36f.). More probably, however, as
already suggested, the fact that Jesus had commented on
the use of the term 'Lord' in Psa. cx. 1 proved influential,
for here He had suggested that the Messiah was more than
David's Son, and may have implied, or have been held to
imply, that He Himself was the divine Lord. It is not
probable that the origin of the title is to be traced to the
use of ὁ κύριος in the Septuagint for God, and it may be
conceded to Bultmann that the designation of Jesus as
Lord made it possible to carry over to Him passages in
which 'the Lord' is mentioned.[1] Yet, even so, it is
improbable that the movement of Christian thought was
in one direction only. The first Christians read the Old
Testament with new eyes, and as soon as Jesus was
confessed as 'the Lord', many ancient passages which
spoke of the Lord must have been applied to Him.
Septuagint usage is not, therefore, a factor which can be
ignored in stimulating the use of the title. The fact that
in many cases in the Acts it is arguable whether the reference is to Jesus or to God, and, as some have thought,
even in Mk. v. 19 ('how great things the Lord hath done

[1] *Op. cit.*, 123.

for you'), reminds us of the possibility of a transitional and formative stage in the history of the title. Most of all the invocation of Jesus in public worship, exorcism in His name, confession at baptism, and communion in the body of Christ in the Eucharist fully account for the use of the title, and of these there is no obligation upon us to restrict even the last, if we accept the view that the narrative of the Last Supper in Mk. xiv. 22-5 is derived from an early Palestinian liturgy.[1] Without feeling it necessary to deny that the atmosphere of the Hellenistic world may have fostered the use of the title, as an alternative to the designation, meaningless to the Greek, 'Son of Man', we do not need to take a step outside Palestine to account for the confession 'Jesus is Lord'.

The immense importance of this fact cannot be measured. Invocation is next door to prayer and confession to worship. Implicit in the recognition of the lordship of Jesus is the acknowledgment of His essential divinity. We must agree with Rawlinson that 'the cult of the Lord Jesus was inherent in Christianity from the beginning',[2] and must not refuse to face the challenge that 'the eventual formulation of an explicit doctrine of our Lord's deity as the incarnate Son of God was necessitated by the fact that it provided the only ultimate intellectual justification of such a *cultus* which was compatible with monotheism'.[3]

---

[1] Cf. J. Jeremias, *Die Abendmahlsworte Jesu* (2nd. ed., 1949), 88-98.

[2] *Op. cit.*, 236.

[3] *Op. cit.*, 237. Rawlinson cites J. Weiss (cf. *The History of Primitive Christianity*, 741) who in a valuable note says, 'The adoption of the Kyrios title presupposes a cultus-certainly; but the cultus presupposes a religious reverence as already existing in some sense', and adds as the only possible explanation 'the assumption that the religious veneration of Jesus was already present in essence in the earliest church'. Rawlinson also refers to E. Meyer, *Ursprung und Anfänge des Christentums*, iii. 218*n*, and to Deissmann, *Paulus* (2nd. ed.), 90, 98ff.

X

THE SON OF GOD

IN contrast with 'Son of Man', which is used by Jesus exclusively, and 'the Lord' used of Him by the believing community, 'Son of God' is a title employed on both sides. With advantage we may include in the discussion the analogous names 'the Son', 'His Son', 'a Son', 'my Son', 'My Beloved Son', and 'the (or, 'His') Only begotten Son'. By this terminology Jesus seeks to describe His relation to God. The same is true also of the community. Whereas in ὁ κύριος, it defines its relation to Him, in ὁ υἱὸς τοῦ θεοῦ it describes His divine status.

I

In New Testament times this terminology had its counterpart both in the Old Testament and in Hellenistic religious usage; and it is necessary to consider first its significance in these two realms.

In the Old Testament 'Son of God' has several meanings. Thus, it is used to describe angels in Gen. vi. 2, where 'the sons of God' and 'the daughters of men' are mentioned, and in Job. i. 6 and xxxviii. 7. It is also used of Israel in Hos. xi. 1, 'When Israel was a child, then I loved him, and called my son out of Egypt', and Ex. iv. 22, 'Israel is my son, my firstborn'. Again, it is used of the king in 2 Sam. vii. 14, 'I will be his father, and he shall be my son', and in Psa. ii. 7:

> 'The Lord said unto me, Thou art **my son:**
> This day have I begotten thee',

52

and by implication in Psa. lxxxix. 26f.:

> 'He shall cry unto me, Thou art my father,
> My God, and the rock of my salvation.
> I will also make him my firstborn,
> The highest of the kings of the earth'.

Further, the term is used to describe the righteous, the true Israel, in Sir. iv. 10:

> 'Be as a father unto the fatherless,
> And instead of a husband unto their mother:
> So shalt thou be as a son of the Most High,
> And he shall love thee more than thy mother doth',

and in the Psalms of Solomon, xiii. 8, xvii. 30, and xviii. 4:

> 'For he correcteth the righteous as a beloved son,
> And his chastisement is as that of a firstborn',

> 'For he shall know them, that they are all sons of their God,
> And he shall divide them according to their tribes upon the land',

> 'The chastisement is upon us as (upon) a first-born, only-begotten son,
> To turn back the obedient soul from folly (that is wrought) in ignorance'.

Since G. Dalman's discussion of ὁ υἱὸς τοῦ θεοῦ,[1] there has been a general tendency to deny that the title was used of the Messiah, or at least to regard the usage as uncertain.[2] It is possible, however, that in the time of Christ Psa. ii. 7 was interpreted Messianically in certain circles, as Mk. xii. 35-7 and xiv. 61 suggest,[3] and the possibility must be allowed that, in reaction to Christian

---

[1] *The Words of Jesus* (Eng. Tr.), 268-89.

[2] In 4 Ezra vii. 28 'my Son, the Messiah' (Lat. *Iesus*) is probably not original, since 'my Son' is omitted in aeth. arm. and Ar². In 29 aeth. reads 'my Servant'.

[3] For Rabbinic teaching *v.* Billerbeck, iii. 15-22.

interpretations, the Rabbis tended to explain Psa. ii. 7 otherwise. The significance of the phrase in Jewish thought is reasonably clear; it does not describe a divine being, but characterises groups or individuals who stand in a peculiarly close religious relationship with God.

In the Hellenistic world of the first century A.D. the title already had a long history behind it in Babylonian and Egyptian usage. The kings of Egypt were believed to be the descendants of the god Ra, and the Ptolemies claimed divine honours, being described by such epithets as *a diis genitus, filius Isidis et Osiris,* υἱὸς τοῦ ʿΗλίου, θεὸς ἐκ θεοῦ καὶ θεᾶς.[1] Similar phrases are used of the Roman Emperors, Caligula, Domitian, and Hadrian. Deissmann quotes inscriptions from Pergamum, Magnesia, and Tarsus in which Augustus and his successors are called *son of God,* θεοῦ υἱός, a translation of the Latin *divi filius.*[2] Strange to Jewish thought, with its strong emphasis on monotheism, the idea of 'divine men' (θεῖοι ἄνδρες) or 'sons of god' (υἱοὶ θεοῦ) was congenial to the Greek mind. It is therefore possible to argue that, while primitive Christianity confessed Jesus as 'the Son of God' the content of the idea was determined by Hellenistic usage.[3] The alternative, as Bousset[4] observes, is to assume that the first community of the disciples of Jesus took the bold step of using the name, and out of Old Testament statements (Psa. ii. 7) and the tradition about the Baptism and Transfiguration creatively formed the title 'Son of God' in a sense strange to the Old Testament and the Messianic faith of late Judaism. Whether this or some better alternative accounts for the use of the

[1] Dalman, *op. cit.,* 273.
[2] Deissmann, *Bible Studies,* 166f., *Light from the Ancient East,* 346f.
[3] Cf. Bultmann, *Theologie,* 127-32; Bousset, *op. cit.,* 52-7, 150-4.
[4] *Op. cit.,* 56.

title, depends on our estimate of the New Testament usage.

II

The Gospels contain many examples of the use of this terminology. In Q the title 'the Son of God' is used twice in the story of the Temptation (Lk. iv. 3, 9 = Mt. iv. 3, 6), and 'the Son', in contrast with 'the Father', appears three times in the important saying about their mutual knowledge (Lk. x. 22 = Mt. xi. 27), about which so much has been written. This saying will obviously call for discussion later.[1] In Mk 'Son of God' is found five times, in the title (i. 1),[2] the cries of demoniacs (iii. 11, v. 7), the high priest's question (xiv. 61, 'the son of the Blessed'), and the centurion's confession at the crucifixion (xv. 39). In addition Jesus is spoken of as 'the Son' in xiii. 32, twice by the divine voice as 'my beloved Son' in the stories of the Baptism (i. 11) and the Transfiguration (ix. 7), and implicitly in the parable of the Wicked Husbandmen, in the words, 'He had yet one, a beloved son'. To most of these passages there are parallels in Mt and Lk, but, in addition, Mt has the title in the saying on baptism in xxviii. 19,[3] and in editorial passages, xiv. 33, xvi. 16, xxvii. 40 and 43, and Lk has it in the Birth Stories in the angelic announcement to Mary (i. 35). It is manifest that this terminology is rooted in the primitive tradition, even when full allowance is made for later and editorial usage.

In Jn these names are naturally more frequent, since it is the Evangelist's purpose to show that 'Jesus is the

---

[1] See pp. 60–2.

[2] See *The Gospel according to St. Mark*, 152.

[3] There is wide agreement that the phrase, 'in the name of the Father and of the Son and of the Holy Spirit', is the language of a later time, since baptism in the primitive Church appears to have been 'into the name of the Lord Jesus' (cf. Ac. viii. 16).

Christ, the Son of God' (xx. 31). 'Son of God' is found
five times: in the words of the Baptist (i. 34), of Nathanael
(i . 49), of Martha (xi. 27), of the Jews (xix. 7), and of the
Evangelist himself (xx. 31); and, in addition, it appears
in three sayings: v. 25, 'The hour cometh, and now is,
when the dead shall hear the voice of the Son of God';
x. 36, 'Do you say ... You are blaspheming; because I
said, I am the Son of God?'; and xi. 4, 'This sickness is
not unto death, but for the glory of God, that the Son of
God may be glorified thereby'. The Evangelist also has
the fuller expression, 'the (his) only begotten Son (of God)',
three times, in i. 18,[1] iii. 16, and iii. 18. His preference,
however, is for the phrase 'the Son', which he uses no less
than sixteen times in sayings, in iii. 17, 35, 36 (*bis*),
v. 19, 20, 21, 22, 23 (*bis*), 26, vi. 40, viii. 36, xiv. 13,
xvi. 1 (*bis*).[2] The usage is interpretative, reflecting the
theology of the Evangelist and of Ephesus; but it is
interpretation based on tradition, as the Synoptic evidence
shows; it is founded upon the knowledge that Jesus had
spoken of Himself as 'the Son' in a pre-eminent sense.

In considering this terminology, we must also bear in
mind the sayings in which Jesus speaks of 'the Father' and
'my Father', for they appear in all the Gospel sources, and
in an intimate sense which transcends that which is
implied when believers are in question. Sayings of this
kind include Mk. xiv. 36 ('Abba, Father'); in Q,
Lk. x. 22 = Mt. xi. 27;[3] in M, Mt. xv. 13, xvi. 17,
xviii. 10, 14,19, 35, xxv. 34, xxvi. 53; in L, Lk. xxii. 29,
xxiii. 34, 46, xxiv. 49: and in the Birth Stories, Lk. ii. 49.
The sayings in M, and still more those in Jn, point to a

---

[1] The alternative reading, 'God only begotten', is read by אּ B C* L 33
et pler. sy^{pe} Clem. Alex. Orig. Epiph. See Hort, *Two Dissertations, in loc.,*
Bernard, 31, Hoskyns, 151f.

[2] In xvii. 1 'thy Son'.

[3] In his parallel to Mt. x. 32f. Luke has 'the angels of God' (xii. 8f.).

development in the tradition. Nevertheless, this type of saying goes back to Jesus Himself and is a correlative to His self-designation as 'the Son'.

In the Acts, the Epistles, and the Apocalypse the use of these names is remarkable. In extent they are much rarer than the use of the term 'the Lord', and their distribution is significant. None of the phrases in question is found in the Pastoral Epistles, in James, 1 Peter, 2 Peter,[1] 3 John, and Jude, and there is only a single example in the Apocalypse, in the words, 'These things saith the Son of God' (ii. 18). There are also only two examples in the Acts, in ix. 20, where it is said that at Damascus St. Paul preached that Jesus is 'the Son of God', and xiii. 33, where Psa. ii. 7, 'Thou art my Son', is quoted. The writers who use this terminology are St. Paul,[2] the author of Hebrews,[3] and the writer of 1 and 2 John.[4] The two last named writers show a decided preference for it,[5] whereas St. Paul uses the Kyrios-titles eight times as frequently.[6] These striking facts can only mean that, while the titles 'the Son' and 'His Son' were quite familiar to the primitive communities, they were associated with teaching more than with worship. The first Christians fervently believed in 'the Son', but they invoked 'the Lord'.

The usage shows that the interests are doctrinal. St. Paul speaks of Christ as declared to be 'the Son of God' with power by the Resurrection (Rom. i. 4). It is as such that He was preached (2 Cor. i. 19), is the object of faith

[1] In 2 Pet. i. 17 the words of the divine voice at the Transfiguration 'This is my beloved Son, in whom I am well pleased', are quoted.

[2] 'The Son of God' (4), 'His Son' (11), 'The Son' (2).

[3] 'The Son of God' (4), 'The Son' (1), 'a Son' (5), 'My Son' (2).

[4] 'The Son of God' (7), 'The Son of the Father' (1), 'His Son' (8), 'The Son' (7), 'His only begotten Son' (1).

[5] Heb has the Kryios-titles three times only, 1-3 Jn never.

[6] Some 130 times as compared with 17.

(Gal. ii. 20), and the goal of Christian attainment (Eph. iv. 13). The 'Gospel of God' concerns 'His Son' (Rom. i. 3, 9), through whose death men are reconciled to Him (Rom. v. 10). God spared not (Rom. viii. 32), but sent (Rom. viii. 3, Gal. iv. 4, 6), 'His Son', who was also revealed in himself (Gal. i 16). To His image those who are called are to be conformed (Rom. viii. 29), and with Him they are to enjoy fellowship (1 Cor. i. 9), while they await His Coming (1 Thess. i. 10). 'The Son' is the object of God's love (Col. i. 13), and to Him finally He will subject Himself, that God may be all in all (1 Cor. xv. 28). Here is not the language of mystical communion, but of objective doctrinal statement.[1] The same doctrinal interest displays itself in the Epistle to the Hebrews,[2] as also in the Johannine Epistles. Here the 'mystical' element is greater,[3] but there are three times as many passages in which the doctrinal emphasis is manifest.[4]

---

[1] This is not said in forgetfulness of the fact that there is a mystical element in Pauline teaching, but this 'fellowship-mysticism' 'far from meaning absorption into the divine, carries with it an enhanced and enriched personality, with increased powers and possibilities of life', V. Taylor, *Forgiveness and Reconciliation*, 118.

[2] There is a formal ring in the description of 'the great priest' as 'Jesus, the Son of God' (iv. 14) and of Melchizedek as 'made like unto the Son of God' (vii. 3), and also in the references to crucifying 'the Son of God' afresh (vi. 6) and treading Him underfoot (x. 29). So too in i. 8, 'But of the Son he saith', while the five allusions to 'a Son' (i. 2, 5, iii. 6, v. 8, vii. 28) express a tone of wonder. The remaining two passages are quotations of Psa. ii. 7, 'Thou art my Son' (i. 5, v. 5).

[3] In the claim that 'he that hath the Son hath life' (1 Jn. v. 12 (*bis*), cf. 2 Jn. 9), the statement that eternal life is 'in his Son' (1 Jn. v. 11), and the reference to fellowship 'with the Father, and with his Son' (1 Jn. i. 3, cf. 1 Jn. ii. 24).

[4] In the passages which speak of 'the Son' or 'His Son' as manifested (1 Jn. iii. 8, cf. ii. 23, v. 20), confessed (1 Jn. ii. 23*b*, iv. 15), denied (1 Jn. ii. 22 (*bis*), 23a), and as the object of faith (1 Jn. v. 5, 10, 13); as the One who was sent (1 Jn. iv. 9, 10, 14) and to whom God bears witness (1 Jn. v. 9f.), whose blood 'cleanses us from all sin' (1 Jn. i. 7) and who, with the Father, bestows grace, mercy, and peace (2 Jn. 3).

III

We return to the question whether the terminology of Sonship and its ideas are native to Christianity, or whether they were introduced into it from a Hellenistic milieu.

The date to which we can trace these titles bears upon this issue. Their use in the Pauline Epistles proves that they were current in primitive Christianity as early as A.D. 40-50 and probably earlier. In this respect the situation is the same as in the case of the Kyrios-titles. But 'Son of God', 'the Son', and 'My Son', as the Gospels testify, are not post-Resurrection titles, comparable with ὁ κύριος, but names used during the ministry of Jesus. If so, they were familiar to the primitive community before there was any contact at all with the Greek world. Even when the Gospel-sayings are held to reflect later ideas, it is still necessary to account for the fact that St. Paul can say to his converts at Thessalonica, with no suggestion that he is using or coining a new terminology, 'You turned unto God from idols, to serve a living and true God, and to wait for his Son from heaven' (1 Thess. i. 9f.). In this usage Pauline practice is already traditional.[1] In these circumstances, the hypothesis of the creative influence of Caesar-worship is highly improbable;[2] and the same must be said of the alleged repercussions of the Mystery-religions.[3] If neither of these explanations is satisfactory, we must fall back upon current Hellenistic ideas of 'divine men' (θεῖοι ἄνδρες), who claimed to be, or were held to be, 'sons of God';[4]

---

[1] This fact is recognized by Bultmann, op. cit., 50, 127, 130.

[2] So Bousset, op. cit., 151n[3].

[3] The fact that the cult of Attis existed in Rome in the reign of Claudius (A.D. 41-54) does not render more credible the influence of the Mystery-religions at this early period.

[4] Cf. Bultmann, op. cit., 128f.

and, on such terms, the hypothesis of borrowing is hardly
worth pursuing. To affirm, as Bultmann does, that the
usage is Gnostic,[1] is only to darken counsel; for, while the
Gnostic movement was much earlier than was formerly
supposed, and is not simply a one-sided development of
primitive Christianity, the nature and functions of the so-
called Gnostic 'redeemers' are fundamentally different.
Only a superficial likeness to Christian teaching can be
claimed for the idea of the divine envoy, who descends
from the world of light to deliver by his teaching imprisoned souls from matter, fate, and death. The Son
of God, whom St. Paul preached, came to deliver men
from sin and guilt, and the statements made concerning
Him are not mystical or esoteric, but, as we have seen,
robust claims about the divine status and work of a
historical person.

The question of the historical basis of the Sonship
terminology in the thought of Jesus Himself will always
depend on the interpretation which is given to the Q
saying, Lk. x. 22 = Mt. xi. 27, and to Mk. xiii. 32.

The former has been the subject of many learned discussions.[2] Here, only the main points at issue can be
recalled. In Mt the *Jubelruf*, or 'Shout of Joy', is a
poem consisting of three strophes,[3] of which only the first

---

[1] Cf. Bultmann, *op. cit.*, 130-2, 174-8.

[2] Cf. A. Harnack, *The Sayings of Jesus*, 272-310; A. E. J. Rawlinson,
The New Testament Doctrine of the Christ, 251-64; B. S. Easton, *St. Luke*,
164f.; J. M. Creed, *St. Luke*, 148-50; H. K. Luce, *St. Luke*, 202f.;
A. Plummer, *St. Matthew*, 165-71; N. P. Williams, *ET.*, li. 182-6,
215-20; Ed. Meyer, *Ursprung und Anfänge des Christentums*, i. 280-91;
R. Bultmann, *Die Geschichte der synoptischen Tradition*, 171f. 354;
M.-J. Lagrange, *St. Luc*, 304-8; T. W. Manson, *The Teaching of Jesus*,
109-12, *The Sayings of Jesus*, 78-80; W. Manson, *Jesus the Messiah*,
107-9.

[3] E. Norden, *Agnostos Theos*, 277ff., maintains that the three Matthaean
strophes form a unit, inasmuch as they are cast in a fixed literary form
(ῥῆσις) current in the East, and found in Sir. li., the Odes of Solo-

two appear in Lk. The second strophe, which is vital to our inquiry, reads as follows in Mt. xi. 27:

> 'All things have been delivered unto me of my Father:
> And no one knoweth the Son, save the Father;
> Neither doth any know the Father, save the Son,
> And he to whomsoever the Son willeth to reveal him'.

The 'all things' (πάντα) are the contents and implications of the revelation (Mt. xi. 25f.) for which Jesus gives thanks, and which can only be interpreted as the knowledge of God in the relationships of the Father and the Son, with authority to make the Father known. Much more is implied than a tradition imparted to Jesus, in contrast with that handed down by the scribes,[1] or the 'Messianic Secret',[2] or teaching concerning the Fatherhood of God.[3] Ultimately the knowledge implies metaphysical distinctions within the unity of the Godhead, but no such interest is displayed within the saying itself, which reveals a unique, intuitive, and personal apprehension of God.

There can be no doubt that the saying stood in Q, and probably in substantially its Matthaean form. In Lk the only differences are γινώσκει instead of ἐπιγινώσκει, 'who the Son is' in place of 'the Son', and 'who the Father is' as compared with 'the Father'. Two Old Latin MSS, *a* and *b*, read ἔγνω instead of γινώσκει, along with many early Fathers, but this variant is probably a conformation

mon, and the Hermetic writings (*Poimandres*), consisting normally of three parts: (1) the revelation of a divine mystery; (2) the thanksgiving; (3) the invitation to receive the revelation. Some scholars, who do not accept this hypothesis, think none the less that the Matthaean setting stood in Q (N. P. Williams, *op. cit.*, li. 217); others prefer the twofold Lukan form (A. H. McNeile, *St. Mt.*, 165f.; T. W. Manson, *The Sayings of Jesus*, 185).

[1] Cf. Wellhausen, *in loc.*
[2] Cf. Easton, *op. cit.*, 166ff.
[3] Cf. Harnack, *op. cit.*, 298.

to the surrounding aorists.[1]   A more important point is
that many Fathers omit one or other of the two clauses
about the Father's knowledge of the Son and the Son's
knowledge of the Father, or quote them in the reverse
order.   In view of the Patristic evidence, and the claim
that the saying is concerned mainly with the knowledge of
the Father, Harnack[2] and T. W. Manson[3] regard the
clause, 'And no one knoweth the Son, save the Father',
as an interpolation.   B. S. Easton[4] explains the third line,
'Neither doth any know the Father, save the Son', in the
same way.   There does not seem to be any necessity to
accept either of these interpolation-hypotheses.   The
Patristic evidence is of doubtful value because, as an
experiment will show, it is difficult to quote the saying
correctly by memory.   Again, the fourlined structure of
the strophes is against these textual reconstructions.
Further, each line seems necessary to the thought of the
whole.   It is because the knowledge of the Father and the
Son is mutual, that the Son can reveal the Father to
whomsoever He wills to do so.   For these reasons we
ought to take the saying as it stands.

The view that the passage is part of a Christological
hymn formed in a Hellenistic environment, is held by
many continental scholars.   It is objected that nowhere
else does Jesus claim to be the revealer of the knowledge
of God, that the saying lacks the genuine Old Testament
ring, and that it is more akin to the utterances of Hellenistic piety, as illustrated, for example, in Wisd. ii. 13ff.[5]

[1] So Creed, *op. cit.*, 150.
[2] *Op. cit.*, 294f.
[3] *The Sayings of Jesus*, 80.
[4] *Op. cit.*, 167.
[5] Here the godless describe the righteous man as one who professes
'to have knowledge of God', and who names himself 'servant of the Lord'
(παῖδα κυρίου) and 'vaunteth that God is his father'.

and in the prayers and exhortations of the *Corpus Hermeti-cum*.[1] The saying, it is said, has a Johannine tone, in the well-known phrase of K. A. von Hase, it is 'an aerolite from the Johannine heaven'.[2] Inevitably one thinks of such sayings as Jn. iii. 35, 'The Father loveth the Son, and hath given all things into his hand', v. 20, 'The Father loveth the Son, and showeth him all things that himself doeth', x. 15, 'Even as the Father knoweth me, and I know the Father', and xiv. 9, 'He that hath seen me hath seen the Father'. On grounds such as these Dibelius[3] and Bultmann[4] question the genuineness of the saying. J. Weiss[5] describes it as 'a community-utterance', and Bousset[6] and Meyer[7] speak of it as a literary composition. Among English scholars A. E. J. Rawlinson[8] finds the question difficult to decide, and confesses that it appears to him 'to be not impossible for a saying which was not literally authentic to have come to be included in "Q"'.

It may be claimed that, if the saying is not authentic, it is still none the less of very great importance. If it is part of a Christological hymn, it may be earlier than the one quoted in Phil. ii. 5-11. In this case, it must be regarded as the doctrinal development of a primitive Christian confession, and it therefore implies the existence of a community, or of communities, in which Jesus was

---

[1] The *Corpus Hermeticum* consists of theological tractates associated with the name of Hermes Trismegistus identified with the Egyptian god Thoth. The first of the seventeen tractates is known by the title *Poimandres*. Cf. W. Scott, *Hermetica;* C. H. Dodd, *The Bible and the Greeks*, xi-xv, 99-248.

[2] *Geschichte Jesu*, 527.

[3] *From Tradition to Gospel*, 280f.

[4] *Die Geschichte der synoptischen Tradition*, 172.

[5] *The History of Primitive Christianity*, 121.

[6] *Kyrios Christos*, 48-50.

[7] *Ursprung und Anfänge des Christentums*, i. 291.

[8] *The New Testament Doctrine of the Christ*, 263.

known and confessed as the Son of God. But the arguments against the genuineness of the saying are not at all conclusive. The fact that it stands alone in Q, and the claim that it transcends the utterances of Old Testament piety, by no means rule out its originality. Again, Johannine sayings are frequently genuine logia expressed in a new idiom,[1] not creations *ex nihilo*, and it may well be that those I have quoted depend on the Q saying or upon others of a like character. Further, the Hellenistic tone of the saying is greatly exaggerated. Bousset[2] attaches great importance to an alleged parallel in the Hermes-prayer in the magical papyrus, Lond. cxxii. 50, 'I know thee, Hermes, and thou (knowest) me. I am thou, and thou art I'. Here, however, the knowledge is mystical, and it implies the identification of the speaker with the god, and of Hermes with himself. It is the language of Indian religious philosophy in the Vedanta system. We are far indeed from the Synoptic saying. There is no reason why Jesus, speaking in the language of characteristic Semitic hyperbole,[3] should not have said that only the Father knew Him, and that He alone knew the Father, and was able to reveal Him to others. The saying is in line with the development of the prophetic consciousness carried to a higher, and indeed to an incomparable degree. If this view is accepted, the use of the title 'the Son of God' is grounded in the thought and teaching of Jesus Himself.

The second of the two passages already mentioned, Mk. xiii. 32, confirms this conclusion. Here Jesus says of the Parousia or of the Last Judgement: 'Of that day or that hour knoweth no one, not even the angels of

---

[1] Cf. W. F. Howard, *The Fourth Gospel in Recent Criticism and Interpretation*, 215-29.

[2] *Op. cit.*, 48f.

[3] Cf. C. J. Cadoux, *The Historic Mission of Jesus*, 152, 202, 213.

heaven, neither the Son, but the Father'.[1] The genuineness of the saying is assured, since it is improbable that words, in which knowledge of 'the day' is denied, would have been attributed to Jesus unless He was known to have uttered them. Schmiedel's submission,[2] that the saying is one of the foundation-pillars for a truly scientific life of Jesus, stands, and the claim that 'neither the Son, but the Father' is a Christian accretion,[3] must be rejected.[4] The saying shows that Jesus used the name 'the Son' of Himself, not in the sense that angels and men may be said to be the 'sons of God', but of His distinctive relationship to God. Thus, Mk. xiii. 32 confirms the view already taken of Mt. xi. 27, and it justifies, and goes far to explain, the fuller and interpretative use of the name in the Fourth Gospel. It belongs to the self-consciousness of Jesus that He believed Himself to be the Son of God in a pre-eminent sense.

[1] In the parallel passage, Mt. xxiv. 36, the phrase 'neither the Son' is omitted by L W Δ et al. minusc. pler. g[1] l r[2] vg. codd. pler. sy [s pe hl] sa bo geo[A]. It is read by ℵ* B D Θ fam. 13 et al.

[2] EB., col. 1881.

[3] Dalman, The Words of Jesus, 193f.; Bultmann, op. cit., 130; Bousset, op. cit., 52.

[4] See further V. Taylor, The Gospel according to St. Mark, 522f.

SUMMARY

Although other names and titles remain to be considered, it will be of advantage to summarize the general inferences suggested by those already examined. Of these the only names which Jesus indubitably used of Himself are 'Son of Man', 'Son of God', and 'the Son'; and it will be necessary later to consider the bearings of this usage upon His own conception of His person. At present our main concern is the attitude of primitive Christianity to Him, so far as this is implied by the earliest names and titles.

1. In the first place, it is clear that primitive Christianity had a firm grasp of the reality of His humanity. To the first Christians Jesus was a real man who had lived in history at a definite time and place. This fact is implied by the use of such names as 'Jesus,' 'Rabbi', 'Teacher', 'Prophet', 'Son of Joseph', and 'Son of Mary'. One of the most significant facts we have noticed is the persistence of the name 'Jesus' in the Acts, the Pauline Epistles, the Epistle to the Hebrews, and the Apocalypse. Apart from the various combinations into which it enters, it remains throughout the whole of the New Testament period a treasured name which gathers into itself a wealth of love and devotion which it is impossible to measure or assess.

The names 'Rabbi', 'Teacher', 'Master' belong to the historic ministry, but otherwise find no place in primitive Christian usage. Their presence in the Gospel narratives is a tribute to the fidelity of the Evangelists to the earliest tradition, in that they used names which had long been obsolete. These names are a valuable indication of the first impression Jesus made upon His contemporaries; they reveal the attitude of respect and the sense of leadership of which the first disciples were immediately conscious. They point to a recognition of His authority and the consciousness of a relationship which speedily transcends that of teacher and pupil. The name 'Prophet' reveals the opinion of the people, which was retained for a while in some Christian circles, but quickly passed out of use. The name is important because it shows that a close link was perceived between Jesus and the great religious leaders of Israel. In Him, it was seen, prophecy spoke again. Terms like 'Son of Joseph' and 'Son of Mary' have a historical interest, in that they point to an actual person, and not to the subject of a myth, although if the latter name is a gloss in Mk. vi. 3, its significance is doctrinal. Be this as it may, it is 'Son of Mary', and not Son of Joseph', which had a future, for in later Christian usage, it has come to be both the tenderest of human designations and one of the highest characterisations of the divinity of Jesus.

2. Secondly, some of the titles show how fully primitive Christianity recognized that Jesus was the Messiah of Jewish hopes. The frequent use of the title 'Christ', and the much rarer use of 'Son of David', illustrate this belief. There is no one fixed meaning of the title 'Christ' as it is applied to Jesus in the New Testament. In its Messianic sense it denotes Jesus as the One in whom the promises of God were fulfilled in the coming of the Rule or Kingdom of God, and it may be argued that even when it became a personal name something of this significance still lingered in its connotation. The remarkable feature in its history is the manner in which the original Messianic ideas were subordinated to the personal and liturgical uses in the names 'Christ Jesus', 'Jesus Christ', 'The Lord Jesus Christ', and 'Our Lord Jesus Christ'. As I have already argued, the change is due to the strangeness of Χριστός in Gentile ears, and its inadequacy as a Christian

designation, and perhaps also to the manifest reserve under which Jesus accepted the name. But we must now add that the name gains in emotional tone from its association with the name 'Jesus' and in religious significance from its combination with the title 'Lord', while in the phrases in which 'Our' is used, it of necessity shares in the communal atmosphere of these expressions.

The title 'Son of Man' illustrates in its fortunes these changes in an even more striking manner. As we have seen, it disappeared in primitive Christian usage because it was not a generally accepted Messianic title and because the Greek phrase ὁ υἱὸς τοῦ ἀνθρώπου was meaningless to Gentiles. But no title dies without leaving behind it a legacy of influence; and the note of sovereignty in the name reappears in the title 'Lord', and its divine meaning in the phrase 'Son of God'. In its later history it suffers depreciation in the theological use of the name to describe the Divine Christ in His human manifestation, the Son of God incarnate. In contrast, in its most recent history, especially during the last fifty years, its currency value has been increasingly restored; for, while it raises many problems, with consequent wide differences of opinion, the conviction steadily grows that it contains in itself the secret of Jesus concerning His person and work.

In these developments of terminology it is clear that the Messianic idea was the temporary mould in which the significance of Jesus was expressed. Inevitably, the mould was of the things that pass, partly because it was strange to Gentile Christianity, but mainly because from the beginning it was cracked and broken by Jesus Himself. Christology, in the New Testament and without, is the consequence of this situation.

3. Thirdly, in primitive Christianity the complete moral and religious sovereignty of Jesus was expressed by

the term 'Lord'. Used only in the vocative during His ministry, the name attained an amazing popularity because it expressed what He was believed to be in the power of His risen life, and was therefore used in the earliest confessions, especially at Baptism and the Lord's Supper. Aided by the Messianic use of the title in Psa. cx., and by the fact that in the Septuagint it is the name of God, it was used of Jesus in confessions and invocations in a manner which expressed sentiments of veneration and worship. If it is too naïve an explanation of its origin, to explain it as a cult-name transferred from popular Greek religion with its associations to Christianity, there can be no doubt that its intelligibility to Gentile converts fostered its adoption and widespread use. From the beginning its use in Aramaic-speaking Christianity in the cry *Marana tha*, 'Our Lord, come', expressed its corporate as well as its individual significance. For the student of Christology its importance cannot be exaggerated. Far removed, as it is, from later Greek terms like 'homoousios', and the Chalcedonian formula of 'two natures in one person', the attitude of worship which it expressed was bound to lead to theological and philosophical attempts to do justice to its meaning. For this reason the confession 'Jesus is Lord' is the seed of Apostolic and of post-Apostolic Christology, and to-day it is the basic conviction out of which emerges any serious apprehension of Christ's Person.

4. Lastly, primitive Christianity found in Christ a relationship to God that was absolutely unique. This discovery was expressed in the titles 'Son of God' and 'the Son' used in Christian teaching carried over from the usage of Jesus Himself. Believers might truly be described as 'sons of God', but Jesus was 'the Son of God' in a pre-eminent sense. In the New Testament passages

in which this name or the title 'the Son' are applied to
Him it is totally impossible to conclude that it is the same
kind of sonship which it is the privilege of the Christian
man to enjoy. The terminology is similar, but the meanings are poles asunder. Originally Messianic, the title
reveals the Messianic idea in eclipse. Doubtless, one and
the same meaning is not always to be found whenever the
terminology is applied to Jesus. Sometimes the meaning
is Messianic, but for the most part, and even in the words
of the Divine Voice at the Baptism, it is Messianic with a
plus. And the plus is the significant thing. When the
Fourth Evangelist writes, 'These are written that you may
believe that Jesus is the Christ, the Son of God' (xx. 31),
all that is left of Jewish Messianic teaching is the language.
And when St. Paul says that 'in the fulness of the time
God sent forth his Son' (Gal. iv. 4), we have passed far
beyond the idea of a divinely commissioned national
deliverer to the thought of One who comes to our world
from the depths of the being of God. When we attempt
to say just how much is to be read into this terminology
we are baffled; but the reason is undoubted. The situation is not one in which a clearly defined label, with a
meaning known to all, is being used, in its application to
the man Jesus. The reverse is true. A man, revered,
loved, and worshipped is described by a terminology
which bends and cracks under the strain, because it is
being used to describe a unique person, and therefore to
serve an end for which, humanly speaking, it was not
intended from the standpoint of its history. Divinity is
felt before it is named, and when it is named the words are
inadequate. And this situation obtains throughout the
long history of Christology. First the perception, then
the halting words, and then the despairing attempt to
find better words. When at length the decisive word of

Nicaca is spoken, all we can say is that this is the best that men can do. And if it should be given to modern theology to speak better words, more accordant with the thought of our time, we may be sure that our constructions will run but lamely after a knowledge of Christ which antiquates them almost before they are framed. Christology is the despairing attempt of theologians to keep pace with the Church's apprehension of Christ. It is a discipline from which there is no discharge, even though it appears to the historian like the task of Sisyphus rolling up the mountain a great stone which inevitably falls back. The difference is that the theologian is not a solitary figure. Behind him lie the affirmations of the Church and the voices of countless Christian believers. He may therefore believe that, when the stone eludes his grasp, other hands will catch it, and that every age will know better who Christ is, even if the final utterance is reserved for the song of the redeemed.

PART TWO

OTHER NAMES AND TITLES OF JESUS

In addition to the names and titles already discussed there are other names in the New Testament which are applied to Christ less frequently, but which, none the less, are of great importance. They indicate the attitude of primitive Christianity to Him, and, in many cases, foreshadow later developments in theology. Some of these terms are Messianic, not so much as technical expressions taken over from the Old Testament and the Apocalyptic literature, but in virtue of their meaning in primitive usage. Others are Messianic with a communal or societarian significance. Others again are soteriological, in that primarily they are related to Christ's redemptive work, but for this reason are descriptive of Himself. Finally, other titles are Christological in the more technical sense of the term, inasmuch as they give expression to an estimation or valuation of His person.

(a) *MESSIANIC TITLES*

XI

THE KING

THIS title is derived from Psa. ii. 7 and Zech. ix. 9. In Mk it appears six times, in each case in terms of contempt and derision. Thus, it is used by Pilate in the question, 'Are you the king of the Jews?' (xv. 2),[1] in the alternative put before the crowd, 'Will you that I release unto you the King of the Jews?' (xv. 9),[2] and in the further question, 'What then shall I do unto him whom you call the King of the Jews?' (xv. 12). It is also used in mockery by the soldiers, 'Hail, King of the Jews!' (xv. 18),[3] in the inscription of the Cross, 'The King of the Jews' (xv. 26),[4] and in the taunt of the chief priests, 'Let the Christ, the King of Israel, now come down from the cross, that we may see and believe' (xv. 32).[5] It is out of such contemptuous beginnings that the name was rescued by Christian devotion.

Of three additional examples in the L tradition two are like those in Mk: the accusation made by the priests, 'We found this man perverting our nation, and forbidding to give tribute to Caesar, and saying that he himself is Christ a king' (Lk. xxiii. 2), and the soldiers' taunt, 'If you are the king of the Jews, save yourself' (Lk. xxiii. 37). In the third Lukan example, which is connected with the

[1] Cf. Mt. xxvii. 11, Lk. xxiii. 3, Jn. xviii. 33.
[2] Cf. Jn. xviii. 39.
[3] Cf. Mt. xxvii. 29, Jn. xix. 3.
[4] Cf. Mt. xxvii. 37, Lk. xxiii. 38, Jn. xix. 19.
[5] Cf. Mt. xxvii. 42.

Entry into Jerusalem, the title becomes a term of honour,
'Blessed be the king that cometh in the name of the Lord'
(Lk. xix. 38),[1] and this tendency is still more manifest
in Mt. xxi. 5 and Jn. xii. 15, in the quotation from Zech.
ix. 9, 'Behold, thy king cometh unto thee, meek, and
riding upon an ass'.

In the Fourth Gospel there is a marked increase of the
use of the name. In addition to parallels to six of the
Synoptic passages already mentioned there are seven
peculiar to the Gospel. These include the cry of Nathanael, 'Rabbi, you are the Son of God; you are the King
of Israel' (i 49); the statement, after the Feeding of the
Five Thousand, that Jesus withdrew into the mountain,
when He perceived that the people 'were about to come
and take him by force, to make him king' (vi. 15);
Pilate's question, 'Are you a king then?' (xviii. 37a,) and
the reply of Jesus, 'You say that I am a king. To this
end have I been born, and to this end am I come into the
world, that I should bear witness unto the truth' (xviii.
37b). Pilate's exclamation, 'Behold, your King!' (xix. 14),
is also given; his question, 'Shall I crucify your King?'
(xix. 15); and finally the priests' protest, 'Write not, The
King of the Jews; but, that he said, I am the King of the
Jews' (xix. 21), which is refused in the firm statement,
'What I have written I have written'.

It is evident that at Ephesus at the end of the first
century there was an increased interest in the kingship of
Jesus. This fact is confirmed by three passages in the
Apocalypse which affirm the supreme dignity and greatness
of Jesus: 'Jesus Christ, who is the faithful witness, the
firstborn of the dead, and the ruler of the kings of the
earth' (i. 5), 'Lord of lords, and King of kings' (xvii. 14),

---

[1] Cf. Jn. xii. 13. Cf. also the question of the Magi in Mt. ii. 2,
'Where is he that is born King of the Jews?'

'King of kings, and Lord of lords' (xix. 16). This interest, however, was not widespread, for there are no passages of the kind in the Epistles, and the only remaining New Testament example is Ac. xvii. 7, where the Jews at Thessalonica bring against the first missionaries the charge of acting contrary to the decrees of Caesar and of saying, 'There is another king, one Jesus'.[1] It is easy to see why the name is not more freely used. The title was politically dangerous. Further, in view of their favourable attitude to the Empire, it is naturally avoided by St. Paul and the author of 1 Peter, just as, for the contrary reason, it is thrown out as a challenge by the Seer John. Jesus Himself had not used the name, and for Christian usage in general, all that was of value in it could be embraced in the title 'the Lord', with the added advantage of the liturgical associations of the Kyrios-title.

[1] In 1 Tim. vi. 15, 'the blessed and only Potentate, the King of kings, and Lords of lords', the reference is to God. Cf. E. F. Scott, *The Pastoral Epistles*, 79.

XII

HE THAT COMETH

THIS name appears twice in Q: in the Baptist's question, 'Are you he that cometh, or look we for another?' (Lk. vii. 19f. = Mt. xi. 3), and in a quotation from Psa. cxviii. 26 by Jesus after the Lament over Jerusalem, 'And I say unto you, You shall not see me, until you shall say, Blessed is he that cometh in the name of the Lord' (Lk. xiii. 35 = Mt. xxiii. 39). In Mk the same Psalm is quoted in the cry of the multitude at the Entry into Jerusalem (xi. 9).[1] In the Fourth Gospel the phrase is used twice by the Baptist: i. 15, 'This was he of whom I said, He that cometh after me is become before me', and i. 27, 'Even he that cometh after me, the latchet of whose shoe I am not worthy to unloose'. After the Feeding of the Five Thousand the people say, 'This is of a truth the prophet that cometh into the world' (vi. 14), and Martha, in reply to the challenge 'Do you believe this?', declares, 'Yea, Lord: I have believed that you are the Christ, the Son of God, even he that cometh into the world' (xi. 27).

In the rest of the New Testament the phrase is found twice only[2] in a general sense: in Ac. xix. 4, 'John baptized with the baptism of repentance, saying unto the people, that they should believe on him which should

---

[1] Cf. Mt. xxi. 9, Lk. xix. 38 (om. ℵ H e l Or.).

[2] But see A. Nygren, *Romans*, 217, with reference to Rom. v. 14: 'Here we glimpse the idea (the new aeon) in his characterization of Christ as he who was to come'; for as ὁ μέλλων He is the head of ὁ αἰὼν ὁ μέλλων'.

come after him', that is, on Jesus; and Heb. x. 37 (cf. Hab. ii. 3), 'For yet a very little while, He that cometh shall come, and shall not tarry'.

Clearly, the title had only a brief and restricted currency in certain circles.[1] It has a marked eschatological tone, and its origin is probably to be found in the proclamation of John the Baptist, 'There cometh after me he that is mightier than I' (Mk. i. 7).[2] In the Apocalypse it is used of God (i. 4, 8, iv. 8). As applied to Christ, the name passed quickly out of use because its eschatological content was covered by the title 'Lord' (cf. 1 Cor. xvi. 22, Apoc. xxii. 20). Already in Heb. x. 37 it is somewhat of a literary survival. The writer follows the Septuagint version of Hab. ii. 3,[3] but inserts the article before ἐρχόμενος. Thus, the reference to the Parousia is artificially constructed, a clear sign that 'He that cometh' was not a popular title in current use.

---

[1] 'There is no evidence that it was a Jewish or Christian technical term', H. J. Cadbury, *The Beginnings of Christianity*, v. 373. Cf. A. H. McNeile, *The Gospel according to St. Matthew*, 34, 151.

[2] Cf. Lk. iii. 16.

[3] The LXX reads, 'For he will surely come', ὅτι ἐρχόμενος ἥξει. Cf. the Heb., 'It (the vision) will surely come'.

XIII

THE HOLY ONE

Like the phrase 'He that Cometh', 'the Holy One' or 'the Holy One of God' does not appear to have been an accepted Messianic title.[1] It describes a man set apart and consecrated to the service of God. In some early Christian communities it may have been used for a time as a Messianic name, but the New Testament examples are few and uncertain.[2]

In Mk. i. 24[3] it is used by the man with the unclean spirit who cries, 'I know who you are, the Holy One of God'. Here it denotes a supernatural agent, but may be intended by the Evangelist as a name for the Messiah. In Lk. i. 35 the phrase describes the child born of the Virgin Mary. In Jn. vi. 69 it appears in Simon Peter's confession, 'We have believed and know that you are the Holy One of God', and is a Messianic designation. These are all the examples found in the Gospels. In the Acts ἅγιος is used of Jesus three times, twice in the phrase 'thy holy Servant Jesus' (iv. 27, 30) and once in the words of Peter, 'You denied the Holy and Righteous One' (iii. 14). The adjective ὅσιος is also used twice in the Acts (ii. 27, xiii. 35) in quoting Psa. xvi. 10, 'Neither wilt thou give thine holy one to see corruption'. Here Christ is meant.

Two passages remain. 1 Jn. ii. 20, 'You have an anointing from the Holy One', may refer either to Christ

[1] Cf. M.-J. Lagrange, *Saint Marc*, 22.
[2] In the Old Testament Aaron is described as 'the holy one of the Lord' (Psa. cv. (cvi.) 16, and Elisha as 'an holy man of God') (2 Kings iv. 9).
[3] Cf. Lk. iv. 34.

or to the Father'.[1] In Apoc. iii. 7, 'These things saith he that is holy', the glorified Christ is mentioned.[2]

Titles such as 'the King', 'He that Cometh', and 'the Holy One' are worthy of notice, not only in themselves, but also because they show how temporary and restricted usages gave place to the more established and permanent names. The same is true of the next title to be considered, 'the Righteous One'.

[1] Cf. A. E. Brooke, *The Johannine Epistles*, 56. C. H. Dodd's exposition, *The Johannine Epistles*, 53, assumes that God is meant. B. S. Easton, *First John* (*Abingdon Commentary*), 1355, suggests that in 'anointing' there is a play in the Greek upon the name 'Christ'.

[2] Cf. R. H. Charles, *The Revelation of St. John*, i. 85f.

XIV

THE RIGHTEOUS ONE

THIS title is not found in the Gospels, for δίκαιος is used generally in Mt. xxvii. 19, 'Have nothing to do with that righteous man', and in Lk. xxiii. 47, 'Certainly this was a righteous man'.

In the Acts it is used three times in a Messianic sense:[1] in iii. 14, 'But you denied the Holy and Righteous One', vii. 52, 'And they killed them who showed beforehand of the coming of the Righteous One', and xxii. 14, 'And he said, The God of our fathers appointed you to know his will, and to see the Righteous One, and to hear a voice from his mouth'. These passages recall 1 Enoch xxxviii. 2, 'And when the Righteous One shall appear before the eyes of the righteous, . . . where then will be the dwelling of sinners . . .?'. In 1 Jn. ii. 1, 'Jesus Christ the righteous', the word is used, without the article, with reference to Christ's ministry of intercession, but here the term has lost its earlier technical meaning, and the same is true of 1 Pet. iii. 18, 'Christ also suffered for sins once, the righteous for the unrighteous, that he might bring us to God'. The phrase is also used in a general sense in Jas. v. 6 and 1 Pet. iv. 18 of the righteous man.

Apparently, the title was used for a time in the primitive community at Jerusalem. It may have been suggested by Isa. liii. 11, 'By his knowledge shall my righteous servant justify many: and he shall bear their iniquities'.[2]

[1] Cf. H. J. Cadbury, *The Beginnings of Christianity*, v. 363f.
[2] Cf. C. C. Torrey, 'The Influence of Second Isaiah in the Gospels and Acts', *JBL*, xlviii. (1929), 29. H. J. Cadbury, *op. cit.*, v. 364, judges otherwise.

Although it quickly passed out of use, and never became general, it has helped to preserve, in virtue of its place in the New Testament, the belief that righteousness marks the personality of Jesus, thus guarding Christian doctrine against the perils of a sentimental emphasis upon His love.

XV

THE JUDGE

FUNCTIONS of judgement are usually assigned to God in the New Testament,[1] and in Heb. xii. 23 and Jas. iv. 12 and v. 9 He is expressly called 'the Judge'.[2] In two passages only is Christ given this title: Ac. x. 42, 'ordained of God to be the Judge of quick and dead',[3] and 2 Tim. iv. 8, 'the crown of righteousness, which the Lord, the righteous Judge, shall give to me at that day'. If, however, we add the passages in which κρίνειν describes His activity, Ac. xvii. 31, 2 Tim. iv 1, 1 Pet. iv. 5, or ἀνακρίνειν (1 Cor. iv. 4) and κυριεύειν (Rom. xiv. 9), or in which reference is made to His 'judgement-seat' (2 Cor. v. 10), we see how steadily this divine office is ascribed to Him. It is, in particular, a solemn and permanent conviction of the Apostle Paul that 'we must all be made manifest before the judgement-seat of Christ'. If these precise terms are not used in the Synoptic Gospels, the action of judging is clearly portrayed in the parables of the Ten Virgins (Mt. xxv. 1-13), the Talents (Mt. xxv. 14-30), and the Sheep and the Goats (Mt. xxv. 31-46). The activity is Messianic, as 1 Enoch lxi. 8f., lxii. 2f. show; it is the task of a divinely commissioned and superhuman Messiah.

The same functions are ascribed to Christ in the Johannine saying, 'And he gave him authority to execute

---

[1] Cf. 1 Thess. iii. 13, Rom. iii. 5, xiv. 10, 1 Pet. i. 17, Jas. v. 4, Apoc. xi. 17f, xx. 11ff.

[2] Cf. Hermas, *Sim.*, vi. 3, 6.

[3] Cf. Polycarp, Phil. ii. 1, Barn. vii. 2, 2 Clem. i. 1.

judgement, because he is the Son of Man' (v. 27). In the Fourth Gospel, however, the idea is profoundly modified by the Evangelist's 'realised eschatology'. The coming of Christ is itself the decisive eschatological event: 'For judgement came I into this world, that they which see not may see; and that they which see may become blind' (ix. 39). There is no real contradiction when it is also said that God sent not the Son to judge the world (iii. 17), or in the two sayings, 'I judge no man' (viii. 15), and 'As I hear, I judge' (v. 30, cf. viii. 16); for the judgement in question is not a dramatic cosmic event in the last times, but that which happens when men are confronted by His word, which itself judges them (xii. 48). It is a process of separation wrought by the Advent of the Word made flesh (i. 14) into this world of time and space. This moving idea and the Synoptic teaching are by no means irreconcilable, and it is therefore not necessary to cancel the phrase 'in the last day' in xii. 48 (*v. supra*) as a later gloss (cf. vi. 39, 40, 44, 54).[1] Whatever view is taken of this question, it is manifest that judgement, present or future, is associated with Christ in the New Testament and in early Christian literature. This fact belongs to the data for which Christology must provide; for to think of Christ as 'the Judge' implies that His office and person transcend human standards and dimensions.

[1] But see Bultmann, *Theologie des Neuen Testaments*, 385.

XVI

THE LION OF THE TRIBE OF JUDAH
THE ROOT AND OFFSPRING OF DAVID
THE BRIGHT AND MORNING STAR
HE THAT HATH THE KEY OF DAVID

THESE four names may be taken together. All appear in the Apocalypse and nowhere else in the New Testament. Their failure to establish themselves in early Christian usage is a further illustration of the waning interest taken in the Jewish forms of the Messianic Hope. The first is found in v. 5, 'Weep not; behold, the Lion that is of the tribe of Judah, the Root of David, hath overcome, to open the book and the seven seals thereof'. Already, in this chapter, a sacrificial interpretation is given to these names, for when the Seer looks, he sees 'a Lamb standing, as though it had been slain' (v. 6). The second and third names are used in xxii. 16 and are based respectively on Isa. xi. 1 and Numb. xxiv. 17. They show that Christ was seen as the climax of Jewish expectations. Of the former Charles[1] says, 'Our author lays more stress on the Davidic descent than Christ did Himself'. The fourth name, introduced in iii. 7, emphasises the authority of Christ as the Living One set over both death and Hades (i. 17).

---

[1] *Rev.*, ii. 219.

(b) MESSIANIC AND COMMUNAL TITLES

The distinctive feature of these names is that they set the Messianic Lord in the closest relation to His community.

XVII

THE BRIDEGROOM

THIS title is not widely used in the New Testament, but, in addition to the examples found there, it is implied when the Church is spoken of as 'the Bride'. It is important because in Hos. ii. 20 the marriage relationship is used to describe the covenant relation of Yahweh to Israel: 'I will even betroth thee unto me in faithfulness: and thou shalt know the Lord.'

In Mk. ii. 19f. Jesus uses the name of Himself: 'Can the sons of the bride-chamber fast, while the bridegroom is with them? As long as they have the bridegroom with them, they cannot fast. But the days will come, when the bridegroom shall be taken away from them, and then will they fast in that day'. It is also used of Jesus by the Baptist in Jn. iii. 29: 'He that hath the bride is the bridegroom: but the friend of the bridegroom, which standeth and heareth him, rejoices greatly because of the bridegroom's voice'. Further, in the parables of the King's Son (Mt. xxii. 1-14) and the Ten Virgins (Mt. xxv. 1-13) Christian exposition soon tended to see in the bridegroom a figure of Christ.

The same idea is implied in Eph. v. 25, 'Husbands, love your wives, even as Christ also loved the church, and

gave himself up for it'; and in 2 Cor. xi. 2, 'For I am
jealous over you with a godly jealousy: for I espoused you
to one husband, that I might present you as a pure virgin
to Christ'. The same figure is also used in the Apocalypse:
in xix. 7, 'The marriage of the Lamb is come, and his
wife has made herself ready', xxi. 9, 'Come hither, I will
show thee the bride, the wife of the Lamb', and xxii. 17,
'And the Spirit and the bride say, Come'.

J. Jeremias[1] has pointed out that in the Rabbinical
literature the picture of the marriage-time is very common,
and cites the saying in Exodus Rabba[2] with reference to
Isa. liv. 5[3] which declares, 'In the days of the Messiah
will be the marriage-time'. He argues that the fact that
the Song of Songs maintained its place, although contested,
in the Old Testament Canon, proves that its Messianic
significance prevailed and became the dominant view.
The use by Jesus of this imagery illustrates His Messianic
consciousness, and especially His close relationships with
His community. Its retention by St. Paul and the author
of the Apocalypse shows the value set upon the idea in
certain circles of the primitive Church. It is a more
colourful version of the parallel conception of Christ as
the Head of the Church. It contains an implicit recognition of His divine lordship, with the added advantage of
expressing the closeness of His fellowship with the
community and its individual believers.

[1] *Jesus als Weltvollender* (1930), 22f.
[2] 15, 30 to Ex. xii. 2 (43*a*, 29), ed. Stettin (1864).
[3] 'For thy Maker is thine husband; the Lord of hosts is his name'.

XVIII

THE SHEPHERD

THIS name is present in the Fourth Gospel and is implicit in the Synoptic tradition. It is implied in the statement of Mark, after the crossing of the lake, that Jesus had compassion on the multitude 'because they were as sheep not having a shepherd' (vi. 34);[1] and in His quotation of Zech. xiii. 7, on the way to the Mount of Olives, 'I will smite the shepherd, and the sheep shall be scattered abroad' (xiv. 27).[2] It is suggested also in His declaration, 'I was not sent but unto the lost sheep of the house of Israel' (Mt. xv. 24), His command to the Twelve, 'Go rather to the lost sheep of the house of Israel' (Mt. x. 6), and in His saying, 'Fear not, little flock, for it is your Father's good pleasure to give you the kingdom' (Lk. xii. 32). It is implied therefore in the three sources, Mk, M, and L.

In the Fourth Gospel the title appears in the well known words, 'I am the good shepherd' (x. 11, 14), and it is suggested when Jesus says that He lays down His life for the sheep (x. 15), and has 'other sheep' He must bring, and that they shall become 'one flock, one shepherd' (x. 16). His sheep, He declares, hear His voice, and no one shall snatch them out of His hand (x. 27f.); and to Simon Peter He says, 'Feed my lambs', 'Tend my sheep', 'Feed my sheep' (xxi. 15-17). This teaching is a perfect example of the manner in which Synoptic themes are developed in the Fourth Gospel.

[1] Cf. Mt. ix. 36.
[2] Cf. Mt. xxvi. 31, and also Mt. xviii. 12f., xxv. 31-46.

Other New Testament passages show that the use of this imagery is not confined to Johannine circles. In Heb. xiii. 20 Jesus is described as 'the great shepherd of the sheep', and in 1 Pet. ii. 25 the readers are reminded that, whereas they were going astray 'like sheep', they have 'now returned unto the Shepherd and Bishop' of their souls.

The Old Testament basis of this usage is manifest in Isa. lxiii. 11f., Micah v. 2-4, and Ezek. xxxiv. 23ff., xxxvii. 24. The imagery appears also in 1 Enoch lxxxv-cx, in Psa. Sol. xvii. 40f., and in the Rabbinical literature.[1] In Psa. Sol. xvii. 40 the Messiah is described as 'shepherding the flock of the Lord faithfully and righteously'. While, then, we can hardly call the title a technical name for the Messiah, it has distinct Messianic associations. These ideas are the undertone of the New Testament passages mentioned above, which describe one who leads and rules his people in mercy and love, and who saves them at the cost of his life. Without embodying a formal claim to speak of a divine Saviour and Lord, the title is in full agreement with those which openly give Jesus this status and function.

[1] See Billerbeck, ii. 536f. Jeremias *op. cit.*, 32, points out that this language is used of 'saviours' in Assyrian, Babylonian, and Egyptian religious literature.

XIX

THE AUTHOR OR PIONEER

THE descriptive term ὁ ἀρχηγός, 'Author', 'Captain', 'Pioneer', is used of Jesus in Ac. iii. 15, v. 31 and in Heb. ii. 10, xii. 2. In each case Moffatt's translation is 'Pioneer'.[1] It describes one who leads the way for others.

In Ac. iii. 15 Jesus is 'the pioneer' or 'author of life', and in Ac. v. 31 'a pioneer and a saviour'. Heb. ii. 10 declares that it became God, in bringing many sons to glory, to make 'the pioneer of their salvation perfect through sufferings', and Heb. xii. 2 describes Him as 'the pioneer and perfecter of faith'. The different translations illustrate the fact that the name suggests the dual idea of One who is the source of faith, deliverance, and life, and is at the same time the path-breaker who has opened the way to others. It is unnatural to isolate the one aspect of His work from the other. Similar ideas, expressed in other ways, are found elsewhere in the New Testament. For example, the thought of Christ as 'the Head' of the New Israel, and the declaration that 'in him all things consist', or find their place (Col. i. 17), although different in reference and in range, are allied conceptions. Like the term 'Head', the names 'Author' and 'Pioneer' imply that it is He who gives cohesion and leadership to His community.

It is perhaps significant that the name 'the Pioneer' appears in two strata only of New Testament teaching, in

[1] The RSV has 'Pioneer' in both passages in Heb., 'Author' in Ac. iii. 15, and 'Leader' in Ac. v. 31.

the Jerusalem sources used in the Acts of the Apostles, and in an Epistle despatched to Rome by a teacher who for the time being is an exile from home. We appear to catch a glimpse of an item of Palestinian tradition in transit westwards. The name never became a technical expression and did not gain a wide currency, but it indicates the direction of men's thinking in the primitive Church, and it testifies to a valuation of Christ's person which became permanent.

XX

THE STONE

THERE are indications in the New Testament and the Rabbinical literature that the term 'the Stone' had Messianic associations. Jeremias[1] cites evidence to show that in late Judaism the relevant Old Testament passages, Gen. xxviii. 18, Isa. viii. 14, xxviii. 16, Dan. ii. 34ff., and later Psa. cxviii. 22, all of which in various ways are applied to Christ, had already been interpreted Messianically. With reference to the New Testament passages mentioned below, H. J. Cadbury writes:[2] 'These passages show that λίθος became practically a term for Jesus and that the name was associated with prophecy'.

The basic New Testament passage is Mk. xii. 10f.,[3] a saying of Jesus attached to the parable of the Wicked Husbandmen, in which Psa. cxviii. 22f. is quoted:

'The stone which the builders rejected,
The same was made the head of the corner:
This was from the Lord,
And it is marvellous in our eyes'.

The same passage is used by Peter in Ac. iv. 11 in the claim: 'He is the stone which was set at naught of you the builders, which was made the head of the corner', and again in a group of Old Testament quotations in 1 Pet. ii. 7 and in *Barn.* vi. 4. By 'the head of the corner', Jeremias[4] thinks, the stone which crowns the building is

[1] *KThW*, iv. 276f.
[2] *The Beginnings of Christianity*, v. 373.
[3] Cf. Mt. xxi 42, Lk. xx. 17.
[4] *KThW*, iv. 278.

meant, the topstone over the portal, and he maintains that
the building is the Temple, that is, the redeemed community of the End Time (*die Heilsgemeinde der Endzeit*).
In contrast with Mk. xii. 10f., he contends, Ac. iv. 11
looks rather to the resurrection. In both cases a decisive
and constitutive function is assigned to Christ.

In 1 Pet. ii. 6 and Eph. ii. 20 the word 'cornerstone'
(ἀκρογωνιαῖος) is used of Christ. In 1 Pet. ii. 6 the
word appears in a quotation from Isa. xxviii. 16:

> 'Behold, I lay in Zion a cornerstone, elect, precious:
> And he that believeth on him shall not be put to shame'.

The same quotation, combined with a phrase from Isa.
viii. 14, is used also in Rom. xi. 33. In Eph. ii. 20
believers are said to be built upon the foundation of the
apostles and prophets, 'Christ Jesus himself being the
cornerstone'. There appears to be little justification for
the rendering 'chief cornerstone', which follows the late
Latin translation *summus angularis lapis*.[1] Jeremias[2]
explains it in the same sense as 'the head of the corner', as
the topstone which holds the building together and com-
pletes it, and Cadbury[3] takes the same view; but many
other scholars have explained it as the basic cornerstone
which binds together the walls and the foundation.[4]
Apart from allusions to these Biblical passages, ἀκρογωνιαῖος
is not found elsewhere, and Moulton and Milligan suggest
that it may well have been coined by the Septuagint
translators.[5] On either explanation of the word we are
justified in interpreting Eph. ii. 20-2 and 1 Pet. ii. 1-10

---

[1] Cf. J. Armitage Robinson, *St. Paul's Epistle to the Ephesians*, 164.
[2] *KThW*, i. 792.
[3] *The Beginnings of Christianity*, v. 374.
[4] Cf. T. K. Abbott, *Ephesians and Colossians*, 71; W. W. Lloyd,
Classical Review, iii. 419a, cited in *VGT*, 19: 'the primary foundation-
stone at the angle of the structure'.
[5] *VGT*, 19.

in the same sense as Mk. xii. 10f., as referring to the spiritual Temple, the community of the people of God, which is constituted by Christ. All these passages stand in line with the saying of Jesus about the destruction of the visible Temple and the building of the new, attested in Mk. xiv. 58, xv. 29, and Jn. ii. 19.[1] The communal interest is well marked in the two passages in Eph and 1 Pet. In Eph. ii. 20-2, not only is Christ described as 'the cornerstone', but the readers are spoken of as 'being built' upon the foundation. In Christ, it is said, 'each several building, fitly framed together, grows into a holy temple in the Lord . . . for a habitation of God in the Spirit'. In 1 Pet. ii. 5 similar language is used. The readers 'as living stones, are built up a spiritual house, to be a holy priesthood, to offer up spiritual sacrifices, acceptable to God through Jesus Christ'. The metaphors of growth and building are manifestly mixed, but the dominating thought is in no doubt. The new community, founded upon Christ, is to attain perfection through Him. In these passages a high Christology is clearly implied. The conception of Christ as 'the Stone' has strong affinities with the ideas of 'the Son of Man' and 'the Son of God'.

This judgement is confirmed by other passages which describe Christ as the foundation of faith and as 'a rock of offence' to unbelievers. This idea appears in a quotation from Isa. viii. 14 in 1 Pet. ii. 8, 'a stone of stumbling and a rock of offence', and also in Rom. ix. 33, where Isa. viii. 14 and xxviii. 16 are fused together in the form:

'Behold, I lay in Zion a stone of stumbling
    and a rock of offence:
And he that believeth on him shall not be
    put to shame'.

[1] Cf. Jeremias, *Jesus als Weltvollender*, 79ff.

Isa. xxviii. 16, we have seen, is also quoted in 1 Pet. ii. 6, and Psa. cxviii. 22 in 1 Pet. ii. 7.[1]

The common use of quotations from Isaiah and the Petrine allusion to the stone which the builders rejected have prompted the suggestion that St. Paul and the author of 1 Peter drew upon a primitive collection of *Testimonia*, consisting of Messianic proof-texts,[2] such as are known to have been compiled in later times.[3] Alternatively, it has been suggested that the two writers used a strophe from an early Christian hymn based upon these Old Testament passages.[4] On either hypothesis the idea of Christ as 'the Stone' is pre-Pauline. It is probably pre-Pauline even if 1 Pet. ii. 6-8 depends on Rom. ix. 33. Influenced by their knowledge of Christ, as both accepted and rejected by men, the first Christians saw in Him the stone of which the Old Testament writers had spoken.

Relevant in the same connexion is the saying attached by St. Luke after the quotation of Psa. cxviii. 22 in his version of the Markan parable of the Wicked Husbandmen: 'Every one that falleth on that stone shall be broken in pieces; but on whomsoever it shall fall, it will scatter him as dust' (Lk. xx. 18). The first part of this saying is dependent either on Isa. viii. 14[5] or on a current maxim or proverb;[6] the second part is coloured by the dream-

---

[1] *V. supra.*

[2] Cf. Sanday and Headlam, *Rom.*, 281f.; J. Rendel Harris, *Testimonia*, i. 30f.; Cadbury, *op. cit.*, 373.

[3] See Justin Martyr, *Dial. c. Trypho*, xxxiv. 2, xxxvi. 1, *c.* 4, cxxvi. 1; Cyprian, *Test.*, ii. 16f., *Quod idem et lapis dictus est*, where Isa. xxviii. 16 and Psa. cxviii. 22-6*a* are quoted together; Aphraates, *Hom.*, i. 6f.

[4] Cf. E. G. Selwyn, *The First Epistle of St. Peter*, 273-7.

[5] So Lagrange, *St. Luc*, 511f.; Plummer, *St. Luke*, 462; Creed, *St. Luke*, 246.

[6] Cf. J. R. Harris, *Testimonies*, ii. 96; Jeremias, *KThW*, iv. 279; B. S. Easton, *St. Luke*, 294.

vision in Dan. ii. 28-49, especially the reference to the stone which smote the feet of the image and broke them in pieces and itself became a great mountain filling the whole earth.[1] This vision was interpretated by the Rabbinical writers with reference to the Messiah.[2] It is probable that the strange Lukan saying reflects our Lord's Messianic consciousness, and takes its place along with Mk. xii. 10f. and the later developments manifest in Rom. ix. 33 and 1 Pet. ii. 6-8.[3]

1 Cor. x. 4 is a passage of a similar order. Here St. Paul makes use of the Rabbinical legend of the rock which followed the Israelites in the wilderness, and says, 'And the rock was Christ'. These words suggest His pre-existence,[4] and the context, which states that the fathers 'all drank the same spiritual rock', directly implies that He is the giver of life. St. Paul does not develop this teaching, for it is not necessary to his immediate purpose, but it receives a parallel development in the Fourth Gospel in vii. 37, 'If any man thirst, let him come unto me, and drink' (cf. iv. 14), a saying which the Evangelist connects with the great day of the Feast of Tabernacles and interprets with reference to the gift of the Holy Spirit (vii. 39). When he represents some of the multitude as saying, 'This is of a truth the prophet' (vii. 40), he shows that he has in mind the smiting of the rock at Horeb (Ex. xvii. 6)[5] and looks upon Jesus as the second and greater Moses. Nor

---

1 Cf. Bornkamm, *KThW*, iv. 284f.; Jeremias, *KThW*, iv. 279f.

2 Cf. Billerbeck, *op. cit.*, i. 877; Jeremias, *op. cit.*, iv. 276.

3 'The images are very confused and probably originate in Scriptural texts dealing with the Stone, that is Christ', Creed, *op. cit.*, 246.

4 Cf. Robertson and Plummer, 1 *Cor.*, 201.

5 Jeremias, *Jesus als Weltvollender*, 44-52, *KThW*, iv. 281f., interprets Jn. vii. 37f. as meaning, 'I am the Holy Rock. I dispense the true water of life, the Holy Spirit', and he supports his interpretation by references to Rabbinical teaching. For this passage see further J. H. Bernard, *St. John*, 280-5.

is this all.   In i. 51, which speaks of 'the angels of God
ascending and descending upon the Son of Man', the
Evangelist shows that he is thinking of the vision of the
heavenly ladder when Jacob slept on the stone at Bethel
(Gen. xxviii. 12f.).

The most important 'stone-passages' have now been
considered.   To these Jeremias adds Lk. ii. 34,[1] which
describes Christ as 'set for the falling and rising of many
in Israel', which in some respects recalls Rom. ix. 33 and
1 Pet. ii. 8.   He also instances the phrase, 'for an example
of those who were to believe on him unto eternal life',
in 1 Tim. i. 16,[2] pointing out that the construction
πιστεύειν ἐπί with the dative of the person is unusual, and
appears only in Rom. ix. 33, x. 11, 1 Pet. ii. 6, all of which
are dependent on Isa. xxviii. 16b.   These examples are
more open to question.   Nevertheless, when all exegetical
caution has been observed, it remains true that an impressive body of evidence shows that in New Testament
times Christ was named and known as 'the Stone' of
Old Testament prophecy.   It is not a question of the use
of a title so explicit as 'the Son of David', but of more
subtle Messianic ideas underlying the sayings of Jesus
and developed more freely in the Epistles.   In this teaching we meet with an original Jewish-Christian ferment of
Christological thinking, which antedates parallel developments in Hellenistic Christianity.   Its distinctive merit
is the pronounced communal significance it gives to the
person of Christ.   As the foundation and founder of the
new community, the basis of faith, and the stone of
stumbling, He is not a man as other men, but a challenge
to the heart and mind of the Church in her vain endeavour
to assess His more than human personality.   As 'the

---

[1] *KThW*, iv. 275, 281.
[2] *KThW*, iv. 275.

Head of the Corner' He gives stability and strength to the new spiritual temple of believers.   As 'the rock of offence' He separates men and judges between them.

XXI

THE HEAD OF THE BODY

CLOSELY related to the idea of Christ as 'the Stone' is the parallel conception of Him as 'the Head of the Body'. It is found in Col. i. 18, and in variant forms in Col. ii. 19, Eph. i. 22f., iv. 15, and v. 23. Similar passages, but without a reference to 'the Head', are Col. i. 24, 'for his body's sake, which is the church', Col. iii. 15, 'in one body' (cf. Eph. ii. 16), and Rom. vii. 4, 'the body of Christ'. Further, in 1 Cor. xii. 12-27 and Rom. xii. 4f. the use of the simile of the body and its members leads to the statement, 'Now you are the body of Christ, and severally members thereof' (1 Cor. xii. 27, cf. Rom. xii. 5). In these passages the relationship between Christ and the community is singularly direct, and in terms of the Spirit the same corporate sense prevails in 1 Cor. iii. 16, 'Do you not know that you are a temple of God, and that the Spirit of God dwells in you?'. The more personal aspect appears in 1 Cor. vi. 15, 'Do you not know that your bodies are members of Christ?', which refers to the individual members of the Church and their common relationship to Christ. The same is also probably true of the eucharistic sayings, 1 Cor. x. 16, which speaks of 'a participation in the body of Christ', and 1 Cor. xi. 29,[1] 'He that eats and drinks, eats and

---

[1] Some scholars, however, think that by 'the body' the Church is meant. Cf. C. A. Anderson Scott, *Christianity according to St. Paul*, 189. L. S. Thornton, *The Common Life in the Body of Christ*, 342, explains the passage as meaning, 'to discern also the common life in the Body of Christ, that is to say, nothing less than the significance of the Gospel in and for the Church'.

drinks judgement to himself, if he discerns not the body'.

The New Testament use of σῶμα, 'body', is funda-
mental to the interpretation of this teaching.[1]   In many
passages σῶμα means the physical body,[2] but in others it
is closely connected with the human personality, the man
as a whole.[3]   Rom. vi. 12f., where 'body', 'your members',
and 'yourselves' are synonymous, is a particularly good
example.   St. Paul, Bultmann observes,[4] never calls the
dead body σῶμα, as Classical Greek and the Septuagint do;
he uses this word when the man is the object of his own
action or is the subject of an event or suffering, as in the
Old Testament use of *basar*.   This is so in 1 Cor. ix. 27,
'I buffet my body, and bring it into bondage', in Rom.
xii. 1, 'to present your bodies a living sacrifice', and 2 Cor.
v. 10, 'the things done in the body, according to what he
hath done'.

It is within this context of ideas that we understand the
Church as the Body of Christ.   It is a living entity in-
dwelt by Him.   In a sense the Church is His *alter ego*,
although we must be careful not to use this phrase in a
way which identifies the Exalted Christ with His Church,
since He guides and rules its life, seated, in the New
Testament phrase, at the right hand of God.   For the
same reason the conception of the Church as 'the extension of the Incarnation' needs to be carefully defined, if it
is not to prove misleading.[5]

In this circle of ideas the Headship of Christ is deter-
minative.   The name 'the Head' asserts His inseparability

[1] See especially Bultmann, *Theologie des Neuen Testaments*, 189-99;
J. R. Nelson, *The Realm of Redemption*, 67-104.
[2] Cf. Rom. i. 24, iv. 19, xii. 4, 1 Cor. v. 3, vii. 34, xii. 12-26, 2 Cor. iv. 10,
x. 10, Gal. vi. 17, 1 Thess. v. 23, etc.
[3] Cf. 1 Cor. xiii. 3, ix. 27, Phil. i. 20, etc.
[4] *Op. cit.*, 192.
[5] Cf. J. R. Nelson, *op. cit.*, 90-100.

from the Church, but excludes His identity with it. As the Head, He unites the Body, renews its life, and directs its functions. This teaching is not illuminated by the Greek conception of the body as a tent or tabernacle of the soul.[1] The mutual relations of the Head and the Body are much more dynamic. The two together form a living organism in the Hebraic sense of the term 'body'. Each part belongs to the whole, and is essential to the whole. Indeed, there is a sense in which each member can represent the whole,[2] while still subordinate to the Head. As the Head, Christ rules, but His commands are operative only in the obedience of the members of the Body. In the language of Eph. i. 23, the Church as the Body of Christ is His πλήρωμα. The active sense of this word, 'that which fills',[3] seems preferable to the passive meaning, 'that which is filled',[4] not only on lexical grounds,[5] but also because it agrees better with the Biblical conception of the body. This view does not mean that Christ, or His revelation, is imperfect, but that He limits His activity by the living medium of its expression.

In this teaching our primary interest is the fact that the Church is the Body *of Christ*, and that in relation to it *He* is 'the Head'. In this title the same communal relationship is manifest as in the names 'the Bridegroom', 'the Stone', and, as we have defined it, 'the Son of Man'. And further, as in these names, so also in 'the Head', a suprahuman person and function are described. In no vital or

---

[1] Bultmann, *op. cit.*, 198f., points out that there are possible approximations to the Greek conception of σῶμα even in Paul, e.g. in 2 Cor. v. 1ff., xii. 2-4, and in 1 Cor. vii. 1-7.

[2] In the examples of synecdoche (*pars pro toto*) detailed by A. R. Johnson, *The Vitality of the Individual in the Thought of Ancient Israel* (1949), 39-88.

[3] Cf. J. A. Robinson, *Eph.*, 42-5; T. K. Abbott, *Eph.*, 34-8.

[4] Cf. J. B. Lightfoot, *Col.*, 255-71; E. F. Scott, *Eph.*, 159.

[5] Cf. J. A. Robinson, *Eph.*, 255-9; *VGT*, 520.

organic sense can any man be Head of the Church; the only tolerable Head is Christ, the Divine Lord. In this title, therefore, as in so many we have examined, a Christology is present in solution; and a high Christology. Given by God to be Head of the Body, Christ must, in the light of His functions, be divine. The necessary attitude of the true Churchman, therefore, is not only that of obedience, but that of worship. As a member of the Body, he must needs bow before its Head, and with this allegiance no other can compete. Still more inevitable is this relationship when it is said that God gave Him to be 'head over all things' to the Church (Eph. i. 22); and it is no more than the logical unfolding of His dignity when elsewhere the Apostle describes Him as 'the head of every principality and power', and declares that 'in him dwelleth all the fulness of the Godhead bodily' (Col. ii. 9).

M

XXII

THE TRUE VINE

THE relation of Christ to His Community is described with special intimacy in the name 'the Vine'. Used in the New Testament only by the Fourth Evangelist in the allegory of Jn. xv, the name appears in xv. 1, 'I am the true vine', and more fully in xv. 5, 'I am the vine, you are the branches'. Disciples abide in Him, and bear much fruit; otherwise, they are cast forth as branches, and are withered, and men gather them for burning (xv. 5-8). 'Apart from me', says the Johannine Christ, 'you can do nothing' (xv. 5). A more vital relationship could hardly be described.

The same imagery was used in the cult of Dionysus,[1] and it is found in the Mandaean writings.[2] This evidence does not account for the origin of the Johannine teaching: but it shows how readily the imagery found acceptance in oriental religious usage. The Johannine usage is rooted in the Old Testament. There the people of Israel are frequently compared with a vine; as, for example, in Hos. x. 1, 'Israel is a luxuriant vine', Jer. ii. 21, 'yet I had planted thee a noble vine' (LXX, ἄμπελον ἀληθινήν), Ezek. xv. 1-8, xix. 10-14, Psa. lxxx. 8-19. Billerbeck[3] cites Rabbinical examples, and in 2 Baruch xxxviff., xxxix. 7 the figure is used of the Messiah.[4] The Johan-

---

[1] To whom the epithet Εὐστάφυλος is applied. Cf. J. Behm, *KThW*, i. 346; Bousset, *op. cit.*, 274.

[2] Cf. J. Behm, *ibid;* W. Bauer, *Das Johannesevangelium*, 183f.

[3] *Op. cit.*, ii. 563.

[4] Cf. R. H. Charles, *The Apocrypha and Pseudepigrapha of the Old Testament*, ii. 501. See also *Didache*, ix. 2.

nine use of the name is, however, in an important sense new, since in the Old Testament the metaphor is always used of *degenerate* Israel.[1] This fact may explain why the Evangelist speaks of Jesus as 'the true vine' (xv. 1), that is, the true Israel.[2] As several commentators have suggested, this teaching may be a development from eucharistic sayings; in particular, from Mk. xiv. 25, in which Jesus speaks of drinking 'the fruit of the vine' new in the Kingdom of God.[3] The Synoptic saying is eschatological. If there is any connexion with it at all, the Evangelist has identified Jesus Himself with the vine, and has expressed the saying 'I am the true vine' in terms of realised eschatology. In it he reflects his own Christian experience and that of the Church at Ephesus.

The saying reveals the close faith relationship between the community of believers and the Exalted Lord. Its communal aspects are even more apparent when it is observed that Christ does not say that He is the stem, but the Vine of which His disciples are the branches. The closeness of this relationship is more completely expressed than it is in the imagery of the body; although here it is true that, while Christ is 'the Head', the Church is also His Body, the Body of Christ (1 Cor. xii. 27). In the use of the name 'the Vine' no such qualifying phrase is necessary. Christ is unambiguously presented as the very life of His community in the words, 'He that abideth in me, and I in him, the same beareth much fruit' (xv. 5), together with the warning that, if a man does not abide

---

[1] Cf. J. H. Bernard, *St. John*, 477; F. Büchsel, *Johannes und der hellenistiche Synkretismus*, 53.

[2] Cf. Jer. ii. 21, LXX, *supra*.

[3] Cf. Bernard, *op. cit.*, 478. J. Behm, *KThW*, i. 346, thinks that the connexion with Mk. xiv. 25 *ist nicht sicher auszumachen*. Hoskyns *The Fourth Gospel*, 555f., points to the close parallel between Jn. vi and xv, and connects both, ultimately, with the words and actions of Jesus at the Last Supper.

in Him, 'he is cast forth as a branch, and is withered' (xv. 6).

The Christological importance of the name is manifest. Its use, and the faith-mysticism associated with it, are not intelligible unless, in the mind of the Church at Ephesus, He was conceived as distinct, in some undefined sense, from the Father who is described as 'the husbandman' (xv. 1). Lagrange[1] reminds us that the Arians concluded from this verse that there was a difference of nature between the Father and the Son. Exegetically, this inference was too crude, but it is sufficient to give point to the claim that the significance of the title is bound up with, and inevitably leads to, the trinitarian discussions of the centuries which followed. If it could be shown that the title was used by Jesus Himself, this inference would be at its maximum; but it is also assured if, as seems more probable, the name was applied to Him by the believing community.

[1] *S. Jean*, 401.

(c) *SOTERIOLOGICAL TITLES*

In describing Christ's work, these names elucidate His
person.

XXIII

THE SAVIOUR

THE name 'the Saviour' was not used by Jesus
Himself, and traces of its presence in the Gospel
tradition are few and of late date. The only
Synoptic example is Lk. ii. 11, in the angelic message to
the shepherds, where Jesus is described as 'a Saviour,
which is Christ the Lord'. The idea, of course, underlies
Mt. i. 21, in which the name 'Jesus' is explained in the
words, 'for it is he that shall save his people from their
sins', and it is often implicit in the use of σώζειν in the
Epistles. More surprising is the presence of only a single
example in the Fourth Gospel, in Jn. iv. 42, where the
Samaritans say of Jesus, 'This is indeed the Saviour of the
world'.

Most remarkable of all is the fact that there are only
two examples in the Pauline Epistles, since here it is a
question of letters addressed to Gentile Churches. The
first is Phil. iii. 20, an eschatological passage which voices
the expectation from heaven of 'a Saviour, the Lord Jesus
Christ', and the second Eph. v. 23, which speaks of
Christ as 'the saviour of the body'. In no passage in
which St. Paul mentions Christ's redemptive work does
he use the name 'the Saviour'. Manifestly, there must be
some good reason for this restraint. The same inference

is prompted by the fact that there are only two cases in the
Acts, in v. 31, 'Him did God exalt with his right hand to
be a pioneer and a saviour', and in xiii. 23 where it is said
that of David's seed God brought unto Israel 'a Saviour,
Jesus'. The use of the name in primitive Christianity is
slight, despite the Old Testament passages in which it is
used of God,[1] which are reflected in Lk. i. 47, 'My spirit
hath rejoiced in God my Saviour', and Jude 25, 'to the
only God our Saviour'.

In contrast, a great change is seen in the Pastoral and
Catholic Epistles. Here, with reference to Jesus, the
title is found ten times: in 2 Tim. i. 10, Tit. i. 4, ii. 13,
and iii. 6; in 2 Pet. i. 1, 11, ii. 20, iii. 2, 18; and in
1 Jn. iv. 14. In these Epistles there are also seven cases
in which 'Saviour' is used of God,[2] in some instances in
immediate juxtaposition with the ten passages listed above.
In these late writings it is possible that the name was
taken over from the vocabulary of Greek religion. The
name σωτήρ was applied to the divinities of the Mystery-
religions, to Asclepios, the god of healing, and in Caesar
worship to the reigning Emperors.[3] ' "Saviour of the
world" ', Deissmann observes, 'was bestowed with sundry
variations in the Greek expression on Julius Caesar,
Augustus, Claudius, Vespasian, Titus, Trajan, Hadrian,
and other Emperors in inscriptions of the Hellenistic
East. The exact Johannine term [σωτὴρ τοῦ κόσμου,
Jn. iv. 42, 1 Jn. iv. 14] is specially common in inscriptions
for Hadrian'.[4] Nevertheless, although this influence is

---

[1] Especially in Deutero- and Trito-Isaiah (cf. Isa. xliii. 3, 11, xlv. 15, 21,
xlix. 26, lx. 16, lxiii. 8). Cf. also Jer. xiv. 8, Hos. xiii. 4.

[2] In 1 Tim. i. 1, ii. 3, iv. 10; Tit. i. 3, ii. 10, iii. 4; Jude 25.

[3] See the evidence fully stated in Bousset, *Kyrios Christos*, 240-6; also
VGT, 621f., and Bultmann, *Theologie*, 79f. For Tit i. 4 *v.* E. F. Scott,
The Pastoral Epistles, 152.

[4] *Light from the Ancient East*, 364.

possible in the Pastoral and Catholic Epistles, it is by no means the only or necessary explanation of the use of the title, for behind these writings lie Old Testament eschatological ideas of Yahweh as the redeemer of Israel and the primitive, although sporadic, use of the name 'Saviour' in the Acts and the Pauline Epistles. It is the sparing use of this title for a period of more than half a century which requires explanation; and the explanation which seems most probable is that the use of the name in Greek religion, and above all in Caesar worship, restricted and delayed its currency in the primitive tradition. How otherwise can we account for the failure to use widely a name so rich in Old Testament associations and so naturally related to Christ's redeeming work?

Once accepted, the name became popular, as we see in the late Epistles and in the Epistles of Ignatius[1] and of Polycarp,[2] and in the Gnostic writers of the second century;[3] and it has retained its popularity down to the present day. Although primarily eschatological, the name has rich Christological significance, for the One who is named 'the Saviour of the world', although human in His earthly manifestation, cannot be otherwise estimated than as divine, all the more because His salvation is not only liberation from confusion, strife, sickness, and the entanglements of matter, as in Hellenistic religion, but deliverance from sin and guilt.

[1] *Eph.*, i. 1, *Magn. prooem.*, *Philad.*, ix. 2, *Smyrn.*, vii. 1.
[2] *Ep, prooem.*, *Martyrdom of Polycarp*, xix. 2. Cf. also the *Gospel of Peter*, iv. 13.
[3] See the evidence supplied by Bousset, *op. cit.*, 240f.

XXIV

THE MEDIATOR

THE idea of mediation is deeply grounded in Biblical teaching. It underlies the sacrificial system of the Old Testament and deeply colours the stories of the intercession of Abraham for Sodom (Gen. xviii. 16-33) and of the prayer of Moses for the people after the worshipping of the molten calf (Ex. xxxii. 1-35). Among many examples which might be cited there is special poignancy in the words of Job. ix. 33:

> 'There is no daysman betwixt us,
> That might lay his hand upon us both'.

In the New Testament great sayings like Mk. x. 45 and Jn. i. 29, the figure of the High Priest in the Epistle to the Hebrews, the symbol of the Lamb in the Apocalypse, and the reference to 'an Advocate with the Father' in 1 Jn. ii. 1, all illustrate the centrality of mediatorial ideas in primitive Christianity. One might reasonably expect therefore that the name 'Mediator' would be not uncommon in New Testament teaching.

In point of fact, still less than the name 'the Saviour' can 'the Mediator' be said to be a characteristic title for Jesus in the New Testament. It is used of Him only four times; never in the Gospels, and not in the Pauline Epistles. In Gal. iii. 19f. St. Paul uses μεσίτης of Moses when referring to the enacting of the Law through the agency of angels, and again in the enigmatic passage which follows, 'Now a mediator is not of one; but God is one', a passage, Fricke declares, of which about three hundred

interpretations have been proposed.[1] The four passages
in which it is used of Jesus are Heb. viii. 6, ix. 5, xii. 24,
and 1 Tim. ii. 5. In Hebrews the word is not used in
connexion with His redeeming work, but describes Him
as the founder of the new covenant. The only passage
which speaks of His atoning ministry is 1 Tim. ii. 5
'For there is one God, one mediator also between God and
men, himself man, who gave himself a ransom for all'.

Since this idea is expressed in other ways in the New
Testament, there must be some good reason for the failure
to use the name 'Mediator' more frequently. The explanation is probably to be found in the meaning of μεσίτης.
The word is not found in the Septuagint, except in Job. ix.
33, εἴθε ἦν ὁ μεσίτης ἡμῶν. In the popular speech of the day
it meant 'arbitrator', 'umpire', 'guarantor', 'surety';[2] it
was a legal and commercial expression. It is possibly
for this reason that, apart from Gal. iii. 19f., it is not
employed by St. Paul; as used in the Koine it was inadequate to express the idea of mediation in the theological
sense of the word. In literary usage the meaning
'mediator' is found in late Greek in Philo,[3] who uses the
phrase μεσίτης καὶ διαλλακτής to describe the work of
Moses. It is significant, therefore, that in the New
Testament μεσίτης appears in the sense of 'mediator' in
the Epistle to the Hebrews, which, as J. H. Moulton[4] says,
'has a literary flavour that distinguishes it from any other

---

[1] Cf. E. de Witt Burton, *Gal*, 191.

[2] See the examples cited from the papyri in *VGT*, 399; Burton, *op. cit.*,
190; J. Moffatt, *Heb*, 107. See also Josephus, *Ant.*, iv. 6. 7, xvi. 2. 2.

[3] *Vit. Mos.*, iii. 163 (19), *De Somn.*, i. 142 (22). See also *The Testaments of the Twelve Patriarchs*, *Dan*, vi. 2, and *The Assumption of Moses*,
i. 14 (R. H. Charles, *op. cit.*, ii. 335, 415). J. Moffatt, *op. cit.*, 107,
describes μεσίτης as a Hellenistic equivalent for the Attic μετέγγυος,
and says that in Diod. Siculus, iv. 54, its meaning corresponds to that of
ἔγγυος.

[4] *A Grammar of New Testament Greek*, ii. 24.

book in the New Testament Canon', and again in the late Greek of 1 Timothy.[1] If this explanation is sound, the fact that 1 Tim. ii. 5 is the only passage in which Christ is called 'mediator' with reference to His redeeming activity, is a mere matter of terminology. The earliest Christianity lacked the appropriate word, and late in the day found it only in a popular word on which Philo had superimposed a religious and theological content. Hitherto, other titles had been preferred, and even when it was adopted, names like 'the High Priest' and 'the Lamb' continued to be preferred. All these terms, and the names 'Advocate' and 'Expiation' used only by St. John, belong to the last decades of the first century, but although they are late, they give formal expression to the values which are already implicit in the title 'Son of Man' interpreted in terms of the Suffering Servant, and in the ransom saying of Mk. x. 45. 'Mediator' takes up into itself much that was already familiar to primitive Christianity, but in the New Testament begins its career as a theological word only in 1 Tim. ii. 5.

From the beginnings described above the title 'the Mediator' has had a great and notable history which has persisted to the present day; and of this an outstanding sign is the fact that the name forms the title of Emil Brunner's greatest book, *The Mediator*: *A Study of the Central Doctrine of the Christian Faith* (Eng. Tr. 1934). Christologically, the name 'the Mediator' is even more important than 'the Saviour', just because it is more explicit. In the conception of 'one mediator between God and men, himself man' the Biblical foundation was laid upon which subsequently 'the two nature doctrine' of the Tome of Leo and of Chalcedon was built. The value of these later theological constructions is a problem in itself, not to be

[1] Cf. P. N. Harrison, *The Problem of the Pastoral Epistles*, 84-6.

confused with the basic meaning of the name 'the Mediator' and its doctrinal significance. Of the importance of this name there can be no doubt. As 'the Mediator' Christ is representative Man and has that divine dignity and status which make Him the sole Daysman between God and men. The name is part of the data of the Christological problem.

XXV

THE HIGH PRIEST

LTHOUGH the Epistle to the Hebrews speaks of Christ as 'the mediator of the new covenant', it prefers to use the name 'the High Priest' when it describes His mediatorial activity. The writer uses this title no less than ten times, in ii. 17, iii. 1, iv. 14, 15, v. 5, 10, vi. 20, vii. 26, viii. 1, and ix. 11. 'It behoved him', he writes, 'in all things to be made like unto his brethren, that he might be a merciful and faithful high priest in things pertaining to God, to make expiation for the sins of the people' (ii. 17). He also speaks of Him as 'a priest' (v. 6) and as 'a great priest'(x. 21). His claim is that Christ, who is 'a priest for ever after the order of Melchizedek' (v. 6), fulfils completely the ministry which was imperfectly exercised by the Aaronic high priest in the Jewish sacrificial system on the Day of Atonement, when he offered sacrifice first for himself, and then for the people of the Old Covenant. In the heavenly tabernacle, not through the blood of goats and calves, 'but through his own blood', Christ 'entered in once for all into the holy place, having obtained eternal redemption' (ix. 12), even into heaven itself 'now to appear before the face of God for us' (ix. 24). This belief is the dominating conception of the author, which in various ways finds frequent expression throughout the Epistle.[1]

[1] See further V. Taylor, *The Atonement in New Testament Teaching*, 176f. In Heb. iii. 1 the name 'Apostle' is added in the phrase 'the Apostle and High Priest of our confession, Jesus ', the definite article being omitted before 'High Priest'. The double name is unique. It suggests that He who represents us before God is sent by God and is the final

Although the name 'the High Priest' is used only in Hebrews, the same representation appears in the figure of the Exalted Christ in Apoc. i. 13: 'And in the midst of the candlesticks one like unto a son of man, clothed with a garment down to the foot, and girt about at the breasts with a golden girdle'. Here, however, there is no reference to a ministry of intercession. It is probable, observes R. H. Charles,[1] that in this passage Christ is represented as a priest, 'but this idea', he says, 'is wholly overshadowed by another, expressed by the designation "the Lamb", where Christ is not the Priest, but the Lamb slain'. Elsewhere in the New Testament Christ's ministry of intercession is mentioned in Rom. viii. 34, 'who also maketh intercession for us', Heb. vii. 25, ix. 24, 1 Jn. ii. 1f., and it is implied in many passages in which He is described as 'seated at the right hand of God', that is, as victor, ruler, helper, and advocate.

Primarily, the name 'High Priest' is connected with the work of Christ, but it is no less significant for the understanding of His person. Like 'the Saviour' and 'the Mediator' it describes One who is worshipped and adored, and, in consequence, is divine as well as human. Moreover, while the ministry which He fulfils brings Him into the closest relationships with men, it is exercised 'before the face of God', and so is a service which no man can render.

revelation to men. Cf. K. H. Regenstorf, *KThW*, i. 423f; *Bible Key Words*, 'Apostleship' (translated by J. R. Coates), 30f, 63.

[1] *The Revelation of St. John*, cxiii.

XXVI

THE LAMB

THE use of the name 'the Lamb' is characteristic of the Johannine writings. In Jn. i. 29 and 36 Jesus is described as 'the Lamb of God' (ὁ ἀμνὸς τοῦ θεοῦ), in the former passage as 'the Lamb of God who takes away the sin of the world'. In the Apocalypse the name 'the Lamb' (τὸ ἀρνίον) is used of Him no less than twenty-eight times. In addition, Isa. liii. 7f. is quoted in Ac. viii. 32,

> 'He was led as a sheep to the slaughter;
> And as a lamb before his shearers is dumb,
> So he openeth not his mouth',

and in 1 Pet. i. 19 the readers are reminded that they were redeemed 'with precious blood, as of a lamb (ὡς ἀμνοῦ) without blemish and without spot, even the blood of Christ'. These are all the passages in question, but it is probable that the same figure is in mind in the many cases in which Christ's 'blood' is mentioned.

The underlying ideas of the name are sacrificial, but it would be wrong to suppose that everywhere they are precisely the same. This qualification applies especially to Jn. i. 29. Here the commentators take different views. Some base the passage on Isa. liii. 7,[1] and others on Jer. xi. 19, 'I was like a gentle lamb that is led to the slaughter'. Others again see an allusion to the lamb slain at the morning and evening sacrifice (Ex. xxix. 38-46), or to the Paschal Lamb (Ex. xii), or even to the horned

---

[1] 'As a lamb that is led to the slaughter'.

lamb of apocalyptic imagery.[1]   Amid these varieties of
interpretation the most constant element is the idea that
fundamentally the work of Christ for men is redemptive
and sacrificial.   The same view must be taken of 1 Pet. i.
19. 'The whole passage', E. G. Selwyn observes, 'is a fine
example of the pulpit rhetoric of the period'.[2] 'The reference is to the Paschal lamb, which was connected *par
excellence* with Israel's redemption'.[3]   In the Apocalypse
two ideas are represented: that of Christ as an offering
(v. 6, 12, xii. 11, xiii. 8, etc.), and that of the Messianic
Leader of men (v. 6, vii. 17, xiv. 1, 4).[4]   R. H. Charles
maintains that these two ideas are merged in the author's
mind (cf. v. 6). 'The Lamb who conquers is the Lamb
who has given Himself up as a willing sacrifice'.[5] 'The
Son is a revelation of the Father on the stage of the world's
history.   Hence, as the Father is supreme in power, He
is supreme in love going forth in sacrifice.   Thus the
principle of self-sacrificing love belongs to the essence of
the Godhead'.[6]   This interpretation shows how closely
the work and the person of Christ are related, and that, as
in the other names examined in this section, He must be
understood from the divine as well as from the human
side.

[1] See further *Jesus and His Sacrifice*, 226-8 and *The Atonement in New
Testament Teaching*, 137f.
[2] *The First Epistle of St. Peter*, 145.
[3] *Op. cit.*, 146.
[4] Cf. R. H. Charles, *The Revelation of St. John*, cxiii.
[5] *Op. cit.*, cxiv.
[6] *Ibid.*

XXVII

THE PARACLETE

THE term 'the Paraclete' (ὁ παράκλητος) is used of Jesus once only in the New Testament, in 1 Jn. ii. 1, 'And if any man sin, we have a Paraclete with the Father, Jesus Christ the righteous'. In the farewell discourses of Jn. xiv-xvi this name is applied to the Holy Spirit, with the meaning 'the Helper', 'the friend from court'; but, as used of Jesus in 1 Jn it means 'the Advocate', 'the Intercessor', 'the friend at court'. In Classical Greek and in Rabbinic literature παράκλητος describes 'a friend of the accused person, called to speak to his character, or otherwise enlist the sympathy of the judges (or, as we should call them, the jury) in his favour'.[1] As applied to Jesus, the name describes His ministry for men before the Father, a function comparable to that of the High Priest in the Epistle to the Hebrews, but with a broader and more direct reference. In view of St. John's teaching concerning the Love of God, it would obviously be wrong to suppose that by the phrase 'an Advocate with the Father' he means that, through His intercession, Christ moves the Father to be gracious towards sinners. As the Father, God is gracious already and always. The idea can only be that, as our Paraclete, Christ identifies Himself with us and speaks for us, voicing our penitence and our longing for reconciliation with God. Windisch[2]

[1] F. Field, *Notes on the Translation of the New Testament*, 102. For the meaning of the word see also Abbott, *Essays*, 86, 97; Westcott, *St. John*, 211f.; Deissmann, *Light from the Ancient East*, 336f.; *VGT*. 485; H. Windisch, *Die fünf johanneischen Parakletsprüche* (1927), 124f.

[2] *Op. cit.*, 125.

points out that, although the name 'the Paraclete' is not used in the Synoptic Gospels, the Son of Man appears as an intercessor in the saying, Mt. x. 32 = Lk. xii. 8,[1] on confessing before the angels of God, and in the role of an accuser in the antithesis belonging to it in Mt. x. 33 = Lk. xii. 9 (cf. Mk. viii. 38 = Lk. ix. 26). In these sayings there are points of contact with Rom. viii. 34, Heb. ii. 17f., and iv. 14-16, and especially with Heb. ix. 24, which declares that Christ has entered into heaven itself 'now to appear before the face of God for us'.

Many Christians find the idea of Christ's intercession difficult because it appears to them to introduce duality within the Godhead. It is worth reflecting that a similar problem is raised by Christ's prayers. The difficulty is not fully met by pointing to the conditions of the Incarnation, for the ministry of intercession belongs to the exalted life of Christ. It is better to recognise that the work of the Paraclete on high meets a deep-seated need of the human spirit in its approach to God, and that the doctrine can be expressed only in terms of symbolism. A more philosophical form of the idea might be the claim that there is that in God which pleads on our behalf; but such a statement is vague, and is inferior in religious value to the assertion of St. John that Christ is our Advocate with the Father. Like many names of Christ, this name is pictorial, and we cannot do without anthropomorphic expressions in religion; they are intended to carry as much meaning as they will bear, so much and no more. And the meaning which this name carries with it is the truth that in all our dealings with God, in forgiveness, reconciliation, and sanctification, we have the succour and strength

---

[1] 'Every one who shall confess me before men, him shall the Son of Man also confess before the angels of God' (Lk. xii. 8). Mt. x. 32 has 'I also will confess' and 'before my Father which is in heaven'.

of the Eternal Christ. We do not approach God alone.
So far as the difficulties about Christ's intercession are not
the result of a crude literalism, they are probably due to
the almost incurable tendency to tritheism in popular
Christian thinking, and they are relieved only by an
intelligent apprehension of the doctrine of the Holy
Trinity. It is within the unity of the ever-blessed Trinity
that the Son pleads on our behalf. Intercession is the
mystery of love within the being of the triune God. Such
ideas seem far distant from St. John's pictorial phrase,
which is religious and not theological, devotional and not
philosophical. Nevertheless, it may be contended that
in the name 'the Paraclete', doctrine in solution is only
waiting to be crystallized.

As in all the soteriological names under discussion, this
name has far reaching Christological implications. It
implies a unique religious valuation of Christ. As the
tide moves with the swell of the ocean, so this name, and
the ministry it connotes, reveal the depths of the hidden
Love of God.

XXVIII

THE EXPIATION

LIKE the name 'the Paraclete' the term 'the Expiation' (ἱλασμός) is applied to Jesus by St. John in 1 Jn. ii. 2, 'And he is the expiation for our sins; and not for ours only, but also for the whole world' (cf. iv. 10). It is doubtful if we can call this designation a name or title. Nevertheless, its use by St. John is so remarkable that it calls for special consideration.

Usually ἱλασμός is translated 'propitiation', but, in view of the pagan associations of this rendering, it is preferable to use the translation 'expiation', or 'atonement', in the Old Testament sense of the covering and forgiveness of sins. In an important discussion of ἱλάσκεσθαι and its cognates C. H. Dodd[1] has shown that in the Septuagint and the New Testament these words are not used, as in Classical Greek, of propitiation in the sense of appeasement, but to denote cleansing, forgiveness, and the covering of sins in accordance with the Old Testament use of the Piel verb *kipper*. While, as regards the Johannine writings, he has less confidence in appealing to the Septuagint than in the case of St. Paul or of Hebrews, he holds that the expression ἱλασμὸς περὶ ἁμαρτιῶν does certainly suggest that this same usage lies behind 1 Jn. ii. 2. He maintains, therefore, that the noun involves the idea of cleansing. 'Christ is a "sin-offering", a divinely supplied means of cancelling guilt and purifying the sinner'.[2]

[1] *The Bible and the Greeks*, 94f.
[2] *Op. cit.*, 95.

It may be doubted whether the general reaction against
the idea of propitiation as appeasement has done sufficient
justice to the judgement of God upon sin. If the only ideas
involved in 1 Jn. ii. 2 and iv. 10 are those of forgiveness
and purifying, we should expect the author to use ἀφίημι
(cf. 1 Jn. i. 9, ii. 12), καθαρίζω (cf. 1 Jn. i. 7, 9), and their
cognates. His choice of ἱλασμός suggests that he means
more. Dodd[1] admits that in the immediate context 'it
might seem possible that the sense of "propitiation" is in
place', but holds that the wider context denies this interpretation. The opposite view is taken in a recent article
by the Rev. Leon Morris.[2] Recognising, with Dodd, that
the notion of a celestial bribery is absent from the Old
Testament, he submits that we must not conclude that all
idea of Divine wrath is absent. The Biblical writers, he
claims, while abandoning pagan ideas, 'used the word
group to signify a removal of the Divine wrath against sin
by a process in which God's own holy will had the initia-
tive'.[3] This judgement, I think, is well founded, even if we
think that the word 'propitiation' is too hopelessly compromised by its associations to be theologically service-
able.

These considerations relate to the work of Christ, but
manifestly they bear upon the significance of His person.
St. John himself prompts this inference. He does not say
that Christ effected expiation, but that He Himself is
the expiation. This is a striking and wholly original use
of the word. It is a characterisation of Jesus. It is
nothing less than the claim that, through faith in Christ,
men find their sins covered, so that they no longer rest
under the judgement of God. This idea is closely akin to

[1] *The Johannine Epistles*, 26; cf. *The Bible and the Greeks*, 94.
[2] 'The Use of ἱλάσκεσθαι etc. in Biblical Greek', *ET*, lxii. 227-33.
[3] *Op. cit.*, 233.

the Pauline affirmation that God publicly set forth Christ as a means of atonement (ἰλαστήριον),[1] through faith, by His blood, to show God's righteousness (Rom. iii. 25). The Johannine statement leaves more to the imagination, but it is not less rich in Christological suggestiveness. He who is so described meets man's deepest need because, free from the limitations of His incarnate life, He is the present and eternal ground of hope and the assurance of salvation.

[1] I am not convinced that Nygren, *Romans*, 156f., and other commentators are right in translating the word by 'mercy seat'.

(d) CHRISTOLOGICAL
TITLES PROPER

All the names and titles examined thus far have important implications concerning the person of Christ, but those now to be considered are more definitely Christological in that in them an attempt is made by the New Testament writers to say who Christ is.

XXIX

THE IMAGE OF GOD

THIS name is used by St. Paul of Christ in 2 Cor. iv. 4, where He is said to be 'the Image of God', and in Col. i. 15 in the fuller phrase, 'the image of the invisible God'. An analogous expression, 'the very stamp of his essence', is found in Heb. i. 3.

The word used by St. Paul is εἰκών, and it will be of advantage first to consider cases in which he uses the word with reference to God and man. In Col. iii. 10 it is used of God.[1] Here the Apostle speaks of the new nature, 'the new man', 'which is being renewed unto knowledge after the image of him that created him'. In these words there is an unmistakable allusion to the divine image mentioned in Gen. i. 26, 'Let us make man in our image, after our likeness'. The same reference appears in other passages in which he speaks of man. 'A man', he says, 'ought not to cover his head, since he is the image and glory of God' (1 Cor. xi. 7). 'As we have borne the image

---

[1] Cf. Lightfoot, *Col*, 214; T. K. Abbott, *Eph and Col*, 284.

of the earthy', he declares, 'we shall also bear the image of the heavenly' (1 Cor. xv. 49). 'We all, with unveiled face reflecting as a mirror[1] the glory of the Lord, are transformed into the same image from glory to glory' (2 Cor. iii. 18). The close association of the terms 'image' and 'glory' in this teaching is very significant in view of current Jewish teaching, particularly in the phrases 'the glory of the Lord' and 'the same image'. The same conjunction of ideas appears in 2 Cor. iv. 4, 'the light of the gospel of the glory of Christ, who is the image of God', and 2 Cor. iv. 6 speaks of 'the light of the knowledge of the glory of God in the face of Jesus Christ'. Finally, the idea that the believer is to be conformed to Christ's 'image' appears in Rom. viii. 29. Those who are foreknown are foreordained to be 'conformed to the image of his Son, that he might be the firstborn among many brethren'. Foreordained, they are called, justified, and glorified. Sanday's comment is; 'As the Son is the image of the Father (2 Cor. iv. 4; Col. i. 15), so the Christian is to reflect the image of his Lord, passing through a gradual assimilation of mind and character to an ultimate assimilation of His δόξα, the absorption of the splendour of His presence'.[2]

We shall entirely misapprehend the meaning of these passages, if, in accordance with modern usage, we think of an image as the faint copy of an original, or, as the *Oxford Dictionary* defines it, as 'an artificial imitation or representation of the external form of any object'. This meaning is quite different from that of St. Paul. In ancient thought εἰκών meant more than 'likeness'; it described the essential nature of a thing. Lightfoot[3]

---

[1] Or 'beholding as in a mirror', RVmg.
[2] *Romans*, 218.
[3] *Col.* 142f.

explains the word as both a 'manifestation' and a 'representation' of the reality or archetype; it is, as H. Kleinknecht[1] shows, the reality itself coming to expression. Of course, εἰκών can also mean 'similitude', 'illustration', 'description', as in the papyri,[2] but these meanings do not illuminate the Pauline passages. Much closer is the use of the word by Plato with reference to the kosmos, by Philo in respect of the Logos, and in the *Corpus Hermeticum* of the world and man.[3] Philo, in particular, repeatedly speaks of the Logos as the image of God.[4] It is not necessary to see in St. Paul's usage a direct borrowing from Greek sources. The idea was in the air. As early as the Rosetta stone (B.C. 196) the phrase 'the living image of Zeus' was used of Ptolemy Epiphanes.[5] It may be that in using the word the Apostle was responsive to prevailing currents of Hellenistic religious thought;[6] but as his own words show, his main indebtedness was to Gen. i. 26 and to Jewish teaching which identified the image of God with the divine *doxa*.[7] This teaching appears to have included the idea of the restoration or renewal of Adam's divine attributes in Messianic times,[8] and, as it is used and adapted by St. Paul, it implies the

---

[1] *KThW*, ii. 386.

[2] *VGT*, 183.

[3] See the examples cited by Kleinknecht, *KThW*, ii. 367f.

[4] Cf. Lightfoot, *Col*, 142f.; Abbott, *Eph and Col*, 210.

[5] *VGT*, 183.

[6] 'εἰκών, πρωτότοκος and ἀρχή may all come from Paul's opponents', W. L. Knox, *St. Paul and the Church of the Gentiles*, 159n[2].

[7] Cf. Sanday, *Romans*, 85; Dodd, *Romans*, 50f.

[8] Dr. Matthew Black has referred me to L. Ginsburg, *Legends of the Jews*, v. 113, to *Tanhuma Bereshith*, 6, which speaks of the restoration of the divine light on the righteous in the Messianic age in an exposition of Judges v. 31, and to the new Hebrew scrolls in the *Manual of Discipline* (ed. Millar Burrows), Plate IV, in which line 24 reads: 'For God has chosen them (the 'elect' of the New Covenant) for an eternal covenant, so that theirs is all the glory of Adam'.

conception of Christ as the Second Adam,[1] without the
use of the name.

In using the name 'the Image of God' St. Paul was
attempting to say who Christ is; and his conviction is that
He is not merely a reflection of God, but that in Him, so
to speak, God comes to light and is expressed. Plummer
is fully justified when he writes of 2 Cor. iv. 4: 'This is
one of the passages in which St. Paul comes near to the
Johannine doctrine of the Λόγος'.[2] Some of the names we
have examined thus far are rich in their Christological
implications, but there are few in which we receive the
impression so much of a conscious attempt to answer the
question further, 'Who do you say that I am?'. The
answer is that He is the representation and the manifestation of the divine glory. In His face we see the *Shekinah*
present in visible form.

As indicated at the outset, St. Paul is not the only New
Testament writer to declare that Christ is 'the Image of
God'. The writer of the Epistle to the Hebrews expresses
the same idea in his phrase, ὃς ὢν . . . χαρακτὴρ τῆς
ὑποστάσεως αὐτοῦ (i. 3), The RV reads, 'the very image
of his substance', but the margin has 'the impress
of his substance'. Moffatt's translation is free, 'He . . .
stamped with God's own character', and the rendering of
the RSV is 'He . . . bears the very stamp of his nature'.
Westcott says that from the time of Herodotus[3] χαρακτήρ
is used to describe the distinguishing features of a person
or thing.[4] It is used of the mark on a coin or the impression made by a seal. Hence it denotes 'an exact repro-
duction'.[5] As Moffatt[6] observes, literally it is 'the very

---

[1] See further pp. 153-5.   [2] 2 *Cor*, 117f.
[3] B.C. v. century.
[4] *Heb*, 12f.
[5] *VGT*, 683.
[6] *Heb*, 6.

facsimile of the original'. It is perhaps strange that the author does not use the word εἰκών of Christ, for in x. 1, 'For the law having a shadow (σκιάν) of the good things to come, not the very image (αὐτὴν τὴν εἰκόνα) of the things', he clearly uses εἰκών as denoting the reality in contrast to a faint shadow. Possibly he felt that χαρακτήρ was stronger and more picturesque.[1] Westcott says that there is no word in English which exactly represents it. 'If there were a sense of "express" (i.e. expressed image) answering to "impress" this would be the best equivalent', he observes.[2] The idea of Christ as 'the image of God' is carried so far as to say that He is 'the replica' or visible expression of the Being of God.

[1] For Philo's use of the word v.Westcott, *op. cit.*, 12.
[2] *Op. cit.*, 13.

XXX

THE RADIANCE
OF THE DIVINE GLORY

THIS phrase, which is a characterisation of Jesus rather than a name, is based on Heb. i. 3, 'who being the radiance of his glory', ὃς ὢν ἀπαύγασμα τῆς δόξης. Westcott[1] speaks of ἀπαύγασμα as a characteristically Alexandrian word. It is used by Philo of the universe, of man, and of the Logos,[2] and in Wisd. vii. 26 in the writer's description of Wisdom:

'For she is an effulgence (ἀπαύγασμα) from everlasting light,
And an unspotted mirror (ἔσοπτρον) of the working of God,
And an image (εἰκών) of his goodness'.

The word means 'effulgence' or 'radiance', and 'refulgence' or 'reflection'. In commenting on Heb. i. 3 the Greek Fathers favour the former meaning, the idea that Christ is the radiance or outflowing of the divine glory, the living embodiment of the *Shekinah*,[3] a conception illustrated in the story of the Transfiguration (Mk. ix. 2f.). Probably this is the right view to take. Moffatt[4] and the RSV[5] prefer the idea of reflection, but, as both Westcott[6] and Peake[7] point out, the thought of exact reflection is to be found rather in the clause which follows, καὶ χαρακτὴρ τῆς ὑποστάσεως αὐτοῦ.

---

[1] *Heb*, 10.
[2] Cf. G. Kittel, *KThW*, i. 505; Westcott, *Heb*, 10; Moffatt, *Heb*, 6.
[3] Cf. Ex. xxiv. 16, Psa. lxxxv. 9, Rom. ix. 4.
[4] 'He reflecting God's bright glory'.
[5] 'He reflects the glory of God'.
[6] *Op. cit.*, 11.
[7] *Heb*, 76.

For Christology the claim that Christ is the radiance of God's glory is far-reaching in its range. Peake says that the metaphor expresses 'the derivation of the Son from the Father, and his distinction from Him, under the figure of the radiance which streams forth from a body of light, and gains an independent existence of its own'.[1] The point of the figure, he says, 'lies less in the process than in the result: the Son is the manifestation of God to the world'.[2] This theological interpretation is not, of course, what the writer of the Epistle says, but the meaning of his words when they are thought out and carried farther.

As implying a result, 'the radiance of the divine glory' describes that which can be perceived. The same is true of the name, 'the Light of the World', but simpler as it may sound, this Johannine phrase, by reason of its frequent association with the idea of life, is even richer, in that it describes what is imparted and received as well as seen. Both phrases imply the divine status of Christ under the figure of light, just as 'the Image of God' does so in the terminology of form.

[1] *Heb*, 76.   [2] *Ibid.*

XXXI
THE LIGHT OF THE WORLD

THIS name is used of Jesus only in the Fourth Gospel, but there are allied ideas in the Pauline Epistles and the Epistle to the Hebrews.

In three sayings the Johannine Christ describes Himself as 'the Light of the World': in viii. 12, 'I am the light of the world: he that followeth me shall not walk in darkness, but shall have the light of life'; in ix. 5 'When I am in the world, I am the light of the world'; and more generally in xii. 46, 'I am come a light into the world, that whosoever believeth on me may not abide in the darkness'. Similarly in the Prologue it is said of the Logos, 'That which hath been made in him was life; and the life was the light of men' (i. 3f.). 'The light', it is declared, 'shines in the darkness, but the darkness did not overcome it' (i. 5). The Baptist, it is explained, came to bear witness to the light, but was not himself the light (i. 7f.). 'The true light, that lightens every man, was coming into the world', although the world knew him not, and his own people did not receive him (i. 9-11). In iii. 19 the judgement which confronts men is that 'the light has come into the world, and men loved the darkness rather than the light, because their deeds were evil', and in v. 26 Christ declares that 'as the Father hath life in himself, so he has granted the Son also to have life in himself'.

These sayings interpret the significance of Jesus, and the influences which give rise to them are religious and doctrinal. The contrast between light and darkness is a leading theme of the Gospel and the First Epistle, and no less characteristic is the constant association of light and life. In 1 Jn. ii. 8 it is said that 'the darkness is passing away and the true light is already shining'. With solemn reiteration the writer proclaims: 'God is light, and in him is no darkness at all' (I Jn. i. 5), and his testimony is: 'God gave us eternal life, and this life is in his Son' (1 Jn. v. 11).

Of this teaching, and especially of the statement that 'God is light', C. H. Dodd justly says, 'Anyone who speaks in this way is at home in the religious world of first-century Hellenism',[1] and the illustrations he draws from the teaching of Plato, Philo, and the *Corpus Hermeticum* are striking and significant.[2] But the deepest roots of the Evangelist's theology are in the Old Testament, in the Psalmist's declaration, 'The Lord is my light and my salvation' (Psa. xxvii. 1), and in the great Servant-passages in Deutero-Isaiah (Isa. xlii. 6, xlix. 6) in which the Servant of the Lord is given of God to be 'a light unto the Gentiles'.[3] In later times the Rabbis applied Isa. lx. 1, 'Arise, shine; for thy light is come', to the Messiah,[4] and this interpretation may be older. On the whole, it is probable that these Johannine sayings have been influenced by Old Testament teaching rather than by the utterances of contemporary Greek religion.

We are on more debatable ground if we try to explain the sayings as the *verba ipsissima* of Jesus. 'I am the light of the world' is, I think, a long way removed from the Synoptic saying, 'You are the light of the world', although, it is true, many great commentators have held

---

[1] *The Johannine Epistles*, 18.

[2] Cf. W. F. Howard, *Christianity according to St. John*, 61f.

[3] Cf. also Isa. lx. 1, 'Arise, shine; for thy light is come, and the glory of the Lord is risen upon thee.'

[4] Cf. Billerbeck, *Kommentar*, i. 67.

the contrary view.[1]   At the most, we could not say more than that, under the illumination of the Spirit, the Synoptic saying prompted a still greater claim concerning Jesus. This view is by no means to be accepted in a spirit of resignation.   We gain a great theological asset in place of a doubtful historical liability if we trace the name, 'the Light of the World', to the inspired insight of the Evangelist quickened by his own experience of Christ and by the life and worship of the Church of Ephesus.   The name is the creation of dynamic Christological thinking, and in the mind of Christians throughout the centuries it has been felt to ring true.   It states what Christ is.

This great name was not applied to Jesus in isolation and without preparatory stages.   Such a stage is to be seen in the words of St. Paul in 2 Cor. iv. 6: 'For it is God, that said, Light shall shine out of darkness, who has shone in our hearts to give the light ($\phi\omega\tau\iota\sigma\mu\acute{o}s$) of the knowledge of the glory of God in the face of Jesus Christ'. Here is not, it is true, a title, but fundamentally the same idea which with dramatic realism the Fourth Evangelist embodies in the sayings.   Less close, but still significant, is St. Paul's description of the Philippians as 'luminaries in the world, holding forth the word of life' (Phil. ii. 15f.), a passage recalling the saying, 'You are the light of the world'.   The nearest parallel is the characterisation of Christ by the author of Hebrews as 'the radiance of the divine glory'.   Of the words 'I am the light of the world' we may say with Bernard:[2] 'This is to make an exclusive claim, such as could be made by no other speaker', and, we may add, which could not be assigned with truth or propriety to any other teacher.

[1] See, for example, Hoskyns, *The Fourth Gospel*, 377.
[2] *St. John*, 292.

XXXII

THE BREAD OF LIFE

IT is natural that common similes should be used to supply the names of Jesus, and therefore not surprising that He should be called 'the Bread of Life'.

The name is found in Jn. vi. 35, 'I am the bread of life: he that cometh to me shall not hunger, and he that believeth on me shall never thirst'; Jn. vi. 48, 'I am the bread of life'; and Jn. vi. 51, 'I am the living bread which came down out of heaven: if any man eat of this bread, he shall live for ever: yea, and the bread which I will give is my flesh, for the life of the world'. As in all sayings of this kind, the form is the Evangelist's and represents the experience and the theology of the Church of Ephesus.[1]

The imagery of bread has a long history, extending far back into Babylonian times. Jewish writers took the greatest interest in the Old Testament story of the giving of the manna (Ex. xvi. 1-36). In Neh. ix. 15 it is recalled that God gave the people 'bread from heaven' for their hunger, and there are similar passages in Psa. lxxviii. 24 and cv. 40.[2] These recollections naturally colour apocalyptic forecasts, as in 2 Baruch xxix. 8, 'And it shall come to pass at that self-same time that the treasury of manna shall again descend from on high', and, in more familiar words, in Apoc. ii. 17, 'To him that overcometh, to him will I give of the hidden manna'. Philo[3] speaks of the

[1] Cf. J. H. Bernard, *St. John*, cxix, cxxi.
[2] Cf. also Wisd. xvi. 20, 'Instead whereof thou gavest thy people angels' food to eat'.
[3] Cf. J. Behm, *KThW*, i. 476.

manna as a type of the Logos, and Rabbinical writings[1]
describe the Messiah as the deliverer, the Second Moses,
who will bring down the manna from heaven. A further
relevant factor is the religious significance which the Jews,
like many eastern peoples,[2] ascribed to the eating of
bread. In the days of Jesus the expectation of the great
Messianic Feast in the End Time (cf. Isa. xxv. 6) was
strongly held, as Mk. xiv. 25 and Lk. xiv. 15 show, and
as is implied in the stories of miraculous feeding (Mk.
v. 30-44, viii. 1-9). Undoubtedly, Jewish teaching has
influenced the use of the title 'the Bread of Life'.

Nevertheless, this teaching alone does not account for
the origin of the name, despite the references in Jn. vi to
the manna. Nor again is the name simply a product of
the Evangelist's 'realised eschatology'. The chapter is
strongly sacramental in character,[3] and a more direct
influence on the mind of St. John is exerted by the words
of Jesus at the Last Supper: 'Take ye: this is my Body'
(Mk. xiv. 22), and 'This is my Body, which is for you'
(1 Cor. xi. 24). The Evangelist is drawing upon such
words in the sayings, 'I am the Bread of Life', 'I am the
Living Bread which came down out of heaven'.[4] Christ
Himself, he would say, is the Bread which He gave.
If we ask why he detaches these sayings from the Last
Supper, the answer must be that he is anxious to correct
current materialistic tendencies in the interpretation of the
Eucharist, and to insist that, in partaking of the Bread,
we receive Christ Himself. As He is the True Vine, so
He is the Living Bread.

---

[1] Cf. Billerbeck, *Kommentar*, ii. 481.

[2] Cf. W. Robertson Smith, *The Religion of the Semites*, 224, 226f.

[3] Cf. W. F. Howard, *Christianity according to St. John*, 189, 204f.

[4] Cf. W. F. Howard, *op. cit.*, 205, who says that the Evangelist's words
are 'a development of the words of institution as found in our earliest
record (1 Cor. xi. 23ff.; cf. Mk. xiv. 22-24)'.

The Christological significance of this name is parallel
to that of the titles, 'the Image of God' and 'the Light of
the World'. St. John does not bring out the communal
aspects of the Bread of Life as he does in the allegory of the
Vine, and as, in St. Paul's words, in 1 Cor. x. 17, 'Because
there is one loaf, we who are many are one body, for we all
partake of the same loaf', probably because Jn. vi is not
the right context for this teaching. In this chapter his
interest is absorbed in the endeavour to say who Christ
is and to dwell upon His power to communicate life to the
believer. 'If any one eats of this bread', Christ says, 'he
will live for ever; and the bread which I shall give for the
life of the world is my flesh' (vi. 51). This claim invests
the name, 'the Bread of Life', with the quality of universality, and presents Christ as the One who completely
satisfies the deepest spiritual needs of mankind. He is
the gift of God to satisfy man's deepest hunger, just as,
in a parabolic manner, the manna was bestowed upon
fainting and dying Israel. As such, He cannot be less
than divine; nay, He must needs be the Word of God
made flesh.

XXXIII

THE DOOR OF THE SHEEP

THIS designation also is used by the Fourth Evangelist alone in x. 7,[1] 'I am the door of the sheep', and x. 9, 'I am the door'. To the latter the explanation is added, 'If any one enters by me, he will be saved, and will go in and out and find pasture'. The door is that of 'the sheepfold' (x. 1), that is, the Kingdom of God, of which the Church is the present manifestation. The first passage, which mentions those who wrongly enter the fold or are strangers, appears to have in mind the leaders of the sheep, and the second the sheep themselves.[2] As 'the Door', Jesus alone has authority to give admittance and the power to bestow life (x. 10). 'To be saved'— originally an eschatological expression—is to have the gift of eternal life here and now, and 'to find pasture' is to obtain constant and unfailing spiritual food through union with Christ. The greatness of the claim is more fully expressed in the saying, 'I am the way, and the truth, and the life; no one comes to the Father, but by me' (xiv. 6).

The idea that there is a door, or doors, leading to heaven is one of great antiquity. It is illustrated in Gen.

[1] In x. 7 the Sahidic version reads 'the shepherd', and Moffatt adopts this rendering, but the textual evidence and the section as a whole favour the familiar rendering: cf. Bernard, *St. John*, 352; G. H. C. Macgregor, *St. John*, 237. C. C. Torrey, *The Four Gospels*, 232f., suggests that 'door' is a misreading of the Aramaic original (for 'shepherd'); cf. M. Black, *An Aramaic Approach to the Gospels and Acts*, 193*n*.

[2] J. Jeremias, *KThW*, iii. 179, suggest that x. 7-10 is a later interpretation of 1-5, and that in 7 and 9 the meaning is 'I am the door for the sheep'.

xxviii. 17, in the account of Jacob's dream, 'This is none other but the house of God, and this is the gate of heaven', and again in Psa. lxxviii. 23:

> 'Yet he commanded the skies above,
> And opened the doors of heaven'.

The imagery appears also in Greek literature[1] and in Gnostic writings.[2]   Such parallels are remote from the Evangelist's conception in which Christ Himself is the door.   The same also must be said of the eschatological sayings[3] and parables[4] in the Synoptic Gospels in which the idea of a door is expressed or implied.   The Evangelist may have known the saying from Q in Lk. xiii. 24, 'Strive to enter in by the narrow door', but here the connexion is only verbal, since the exhortation is a challenge to moral effort.   A more probable suggestion[5] is that he is indebted to Psa. cxviii. 20:

> 'This is the gate of the Lord:
> The righteous shall enter into it',

especially since this passage was interpreted Messianically in later times,[6] and, as Mk. xii. 10f. suggests, belongs to a Psalm upon which Jesus had reflected.   We must allow, however, for a development in the Evangelist's thought.   The name arises naturally out of the allegory of Jn. x. 1-5 and expresses his conviction that entrance into life depends on believing in Jesus.   The name is the expression of his spiritual evaluation of the significance of Jesus.

In early Christianity the name appears in Ignatius,[7]

---

[1] Cf. Homer, *Il.*, v. 749.
[2] Cf. Jeremias, *KThW*, iii. 176f.
[3] Mk. xiii. 29, Lk. xii. 36, xiii. 24f., Mt. vii. 7f.   Cf. Apoc. iii. 7f.
[4] Mt. xxii. 12, xxv. 10, 21, 23.
[5] Cf. W. F. Howard, *Christianity according to St. John*, 138.
[6] Cf. Jeremias, *op. cit.*, 179.
[7] *Philad.*, ix. 1.

Hermas,[1] and other post-Apostolic writers; but it has not attained the permanence which belongs to other Johannine titles, partly because the truth that Jesus is the only way to the Father was expressed in other ways,[2] and partly because an even deeper impression was made by the picture of Christ standing at the door and knocking, as depicted in Apoc. iii. 20, especially when this passage was interpreted as His call to repentance.[3]   Nevertheless, the description of Christ as 'the Door', as 'the one means of entrance to the Church at all times',[4] has imperishable value both in itself and as illustrating the high Johannine estimate of His person.

[1] *Sim.*, ix. 12. 1.
[2] Cf. Rom. iii. 26, Ac. xvi. 31, etc.
[3] Cf. R. H. Charles, *Rev.*, i. 100f.
[4] Westcott, *St. John, in loc.*

XXXIV

THE RESURRECTION
AND THE LIFE

THIS name is used only in Jn. xi. 25. More than any other of the 'I am' sayings, it resembles the use of the term 'the Expiation' in 1 Jn. ii. 2, in that an activity or function is used as a designation.

Much has been said already of the keyword 'life' in the Fourth Gospel. Life is that which came into being in the Logos and was the light of men (i. 3f.), shining unconquered in the darkness (i. 5). The promise of Christ is that through Him, as 'the Light of the World', men will have 'the light of life' (viii. 12). As the Father has life in Himself, so has He granted the Son also to have life in Himself (v. 26). Since He is the Bread of Life, the believer has eternal life (vi. 47f.), and the bread which He will give is 'for the life of the world' (vi. 51). He comes that men 'may have life, and may have it abundantly' (x. 10). He is 'the Door', and if any man enters by Him, he will be saved, and will go in and out and find pasture (x. 9). Still more succinctly is this teaching summarized in 1 Jn. v. 11, in the statement: 'God gave us eternal life, and this life is in his Son'.

With such teaching the power of Christ to raise the dead is naturally associated. Four times in Jn. vi Jesus says of the believer, 'I will raise him up at the last day' (*vv.* 39, 40, 44, 54). These phrases are often said to be interpolations.[1] This explanation is not necessary, unless

---

[1] Cf. Bultmann, *Theologie des Neuen Testaments*, 385; Bousset, *Kyrios Christos*, 177n.

we explain v. 28f. in the same way, and regard a belief in resurrection 'at the last day' as incompatible with that present and immediate emphasis which Jesus gives in this Gospel to the idea of rising from the dead. In v. 25-9 the two conceptions lie side by side. In 25 Jesus declares that the hour is coming, and 'now is', when the dead will hear the voice of the Son of God, and that those who hear 'will live', and in 28 He explicitly refers to 'all who are in the tombs', who will hear His voice and 'come forth', some to 'the resurrection of life' and others to 'the resurrection of judgement'. There are too many examples of the way in which the Evangelist can hold apparently contradictory ideas, particularly as regards the idea of judgement, to ensure confidence in cancellations which reduce his teaching to logical consistency; and it is best to allow room for both strands in his thought. While v. 25 may refer to the rising of the 'spiritually dead',[1] his extended treatment of the Raising of Lazarus (xi. 1-53) is enough to show that his theology includes the belief in bodily resurrection. The really distinctive element in his teaching is the belief that, whether now or at the last day, resurrection is implicit in His person; and this belief has become the life centre of the Christian Hope. We no longer believe in life after death because of the nature and constitution of the soul or for any reason at all save belief in the Living God, who has revealed Himself in His Son raised from the dead, with whom, through faith, we may have abiding union.

These are the convictions which are embodied in the name, 'the Resurrection and the Life'. This is essentially what Christ is. And in coining this name, the Evangelist has given permanent expression to the belief that Jesus

---

[1] Cf. Bernard, *St. John*, 242; G. H. C. Macgregor, *St. John*, 178; M.-J. Lagrange, *S. Jean*, 147.

comes to our world from the Beyond, even from God Himself. However responsive St. John may be to the religious thought-world of his day, few will be disposed to suggest that this is a designation taken over from Greek religion. Too indelibly the name bears the Johannine stamp, revealing the Evangelist's experience and the belief of the Church of his day, and its truth is countersigned by Christian experience throughout the centuries.

XXXV

THE WAY, AND THE TRUTH,
AND THE LIFE

THIS name is the most comprehensive of the Fourth Evangelist's designations of Christ, and it is used once in Jn. xiv. 6. 'No one', he adds, 'comes to the Father, save by me'. It has been held that, in accordance with Semitic idiom, 'truth' and 'life' are used adjectivally, with the meaning 'I am the true and living way'.[1] So Moffatt translates: 'I am the real and living way'. This rendering hardly seems necessary,[2] for, as W. F. Howard observes, 'Truth and Life are both key words in the Johannine message of Christianity'.[3]

The name 'the Life' is treated in the last section. 'The Way' recalls the saying in Mt. vii. 13, 'Enter by the narrow gate', which goes on to describe two ways, one leading to life and the other to death, and which probably conflates the Q saying in Lk. xiii. 24 about the narrow door with a version taken from M.[4] The connexion, however, is not at all close, for in the Johannine saying the way is Jesus Himself. There is a closer parallel in Heb. x. 19f., 'Therefore, brethren, since we have confidence to enter the sanctuary by the blood of Jesus, by the new and living way which he opened for us through the veil, that is, through his flesh . . ., let us draw near with a true heart

[1] Cf. J. Lightfoot, *Horae Hebraicae*, iii, 398. See also W. Michaelis, *KThW*, v. 84, who maintains that 'the way' is the over-ruling idea.

[2] Cf. J. H. Bernard, *St. John*, 538; W. F. Howard, *Christianity according to St. John*, 183; RSV.

[3] *Op. cit.*, 183.

[4] Cf. B. H. Streeter, *The Four Gospels*, 283.

in full assurance of faith'. Even this passage, however, is not a true parallel to the Johannine statement, for, while it speaks of Christ as having opened a way 'through His flesh'[1] into the heavenly world, it does not directly describe Him as Himself 'the Way'.[2] The nearest approach to this conception is Eph. ii. 18, where it is said of Jew and of Gentile, 'Through him we both have our access in one Spirit unto the Father'. It is apparent that the Evangelist has taken a new and creative step when he presents Christ as 'the Way'. How great is the step taken is manifest when we recall the Psalmist's prayer, 'Teach me thy way, O Lord' (Psa. xxvii. 11, lxxxvi. 11) or Philo's description of philosophy as 'the royal way', or again the Buddha's teaching regarding the Noble Eightfold Path and Chinese doctrine concerning Tao, 'the Way'.[3] It may be that, as in all the 'I am 'sayings, the Evangelist is using a thought mould current in the Hellenistic religious vocabulary of his day,[4] but the creative and controlling motive is Christological. Christ as known and worshipped is 'the Way'; it is the experience of the Church which is embodied in the name, because Christ has been found to be the living way to the Father. The name elucidates the primary religious discovery.

The third name, 'the Truth', can be understood against the background of the Evangelist's use of the word.[5]

---

[1] Cf. Westcott, *Heb.*, 320; Peake, *Heb*, 202f.

[2] Cf. Bernard, *St. John*, 537: 'This is the doctrine which becomes explicit (cf. Eph. ii. 18) in the words "I am the Way" '.

[3] Cf. Howard, *op. cit.*, 175. For Philo's teaching *v*. W. Michaelis, *KThW*, v. 60-4.

[4] Bauer, *Das Johannesevangelium*, 174, instances the divine leaders in the Hermetic Writings who lead back imprisoned souls to the heavenly world of light, and kindred teaching, much too late in date, in the sacred books of Mandaism. Cf. Hoskyns, *The Fourth Gospel*, 536.

[5] Cf. Bultmann, *KThW*, i, 233-51; E. C. Blackman, *TWB*, 269f.; R. H. Strachan, *The Fourth Gospel*, 141-5; N. H. Snaith, *The Distinctive Ideas of the Old Testament*, 181f.; W. F. Howard, *op. cit.*, 183.

In his use of ἀλήθεια he is indebted both to the Old Testament use of *emeth*, 'faithfulness', 'reliability', and to the Greek conception of truth in contrast with falsehood, or reality over against appearance. Probably the Jewish influence is the greater. Sometimes, when ἀλήθεια is used objectively, it appears to mean God's revelation.[1] Thus, the Evangelist can say, 'Thy word is truth' (xvii. 17), and speak of knowing the truth which shall make men free (viii. 32). He can also represent Christ as saying that the purpose of His coming into the world is that He 'should bear witness to the truth', that is, should be the bearer of God's revelation. When, therefore, Christ is named 'the Truth', the meaning is that this revelation is embodied in His person. This is a highly original use of the name which renders alleged parallel usages in the Mystery-religions[2] dubious, if not merely verbal. The Johannine name reflects a definitely Christian theology.

The full force of these names is perceived only when they are taken together, as the Evangelist uses them. So far from the second and third being subordinate to the first, there is progressive meaning in the composite name. Jesus is 'the Way', through whom, as 'the Truth', we receive the knowledge of God, and in whom, as 'the Life', we have here and now eternal life. The words which follow the three names, 'No one comes to the Father, but by me' (xiv. 6*b*), refer, not only to the first, but to all. Christ is 'the Way' to the Father because He is also 'the Truth' and 'the Life'. This interpretation mitigates the apparent harshness of the saying, but not its exclusiveness. The exclusiveness, however, is fully justified, if the name is

---

[1] Cf. Bultmann, *op. cit.*, i, 245-8.

[2] W. Bauer, *op. cit.*, 174, mentions the Isis-prayer in P. Oxy. 1380, 63 where the word is used with reference to the goddess, and in the 'I-word' in Z. P. Lond. 46, 148, 'I am the Truth'. For other examples *v.* W. Bauer, *Griechisch-Deutsches Wörterbuch*, ed. 4, 65.

taken as one whole; for of whom else can it be said that
He is the way to the Father, the perfect revelation of God,
and the giver of fulness of life? To say, as Michaelis[1]
does, that 'Jesus is the Way, in that, or in so far as, He
is the Truth and the Life', is to justify the most exclusive
claim. The name 'the Word' is the profoundest of the
Johannine titles, but it may be doubted if there is any so
rich in religious meaning as 'the Way, and the Truth, and
the Life'. As such, it belongs to the essential data of
Christology.

[1] *KThW*, v. 84.

XXXVI

THE FIRSTBORN

THIS name is applied to Christ by St. Paul, the writer of the Epistle to the Hebrews, and the Seer John. In Rom. viii. 29 St. Paul says that God predestinated those whom He foreknew to be conformed to the image of His Son, 'in order that he might be the firstborn (πρωτότοκος) among many brethren'. In Col. i. 18 the Apostle describes Him as 'the firstborn from the dead', in close association with the titles 'the Head of the Body' and 'the Beginning',[1] and immediately followed by the words, 'that in all things he might have the preeminence and the affirmation,' 'For in him all the fulness (of God) was pleased to dwell'. Finally, in Col. i. 15-17, along with the name 'the Image of the invisible God', he speaks of Him as 'the firstborn of all creation', and declares that 'in him all things were created', that 'he is before all things', and that ' in him all things hold together'. The name is used also in Heb. i. 6, 'When he again bringeth the firstborn into the world, he saith, And let all the angels of God worship him', and in the greeting of Apoc. i. 4f., 'Grace to you and peace . . . and from Jesus Christ, the faithful witness, the firstborn of the dead, and the ruler of the kings of the earth'. The Christological importance of these titles is manifest.[2]

---

[1] See later, pp. 156-8.

[2] In its more general sense it is used of Christ in Lk. ii. 7, 'She brought forth her firstborn son', and of the faithful dead in Heb. xii. 23, 'the church of the firstborn who are enrolled in heaven'.

This terminology is derived from the Old Testament where it is used of Israel in Ex. iv. 22,[1] of Ephraim in Jer. xxxi. 9,[2] and of the Messianic King in Psa. lxxxix. 27.[3] It carries with it all the associations which were connected with the firstborn in the flock, held to belong to God, and the firstborn son who inherited the birthright and a double share of the inheritance.[4]   It is not surprising that these ideas were taken up by Philo, who, however, uses πρωτόγονος rather than πρωτότοκος, with reference to the Logos.   In the Pauline passages, as Lightfoot[5] maintains, the name assigns both priority and sovereignty to Christ.   T. K. Abbott[6] questions the idea of sovereignty, but as A. S. Peake[7] justly observes, while the word 'firstborn' properly expresses temporal priority, 'the notion of dominion came to be included in it' from the position given to the firstborn son.   The Pauline passages, and in particular Col. i. 15 and 18, imply that Christ occupies a place of absolute supremacy.   This claim is proved, not only by the other names with which 'the Firstborn' is associated in these passages,[8] but also by the great doctrinal statements which are appended.[9]   The phrase πάσης κτίσεως means that Christ 'stands in the relation of πρωτότοκος to all creation'.[10]   The fact that the Arians interpreted the phrase to mean that Christ was a created being led many orthodox fathers to maintain that it

---

[1] 'Thus saith the Lord, Israel is my son, my firstborn'.

[2] 'For I am a father to Israel, and Ephraim is my firstborn'.

[3] 'I also will make him my firstborn, the highest of the kings of the earth'.

[4] Cf. C. E. B. Cranfield, *TWB*, 83.

[5] *Col*, 144f., where references to Philo's teaching are given.

[6] *Eph and Col*, 211.

[7] *Heb*, 83.

[8] E.g. 'the Head of the Body', 'the Image of the invisible God', 'the Ruler of the kings of the earth'.

[9] See above, p. 148.

[10] Lightfoot, *Col*, 146.

describes the Incarnate Christ, and, in consequence, to
explain 'creation' as meaning the new spiritual creation.
Thus, Lightfoot says, 'the strongest argument against
Arianism melted away in the attempt to combat Arianism
on false grounds'.[1] J. F. Bethune-Baker[2] observes that
'all that the phrase can be said with certainty to mean is
"born before all creation (*or* every creature)".' If, however,
we have regard to the context, the name must be held to
imply some form of pre-existence, as also in Heb. i. 6.[3]
The use of the name is a primitive attempt to indicate the
unique character of Christ's person in relation to God,
man, and the universe. The phrase 'firstborn of all
creation' was included in the Baptismal Creed of Caesarea,[4]
but its future was compromised by its ambiguity, and at
Nicaea the inclusion of '*homoousios*', 'of one substance',
was felt to be necessary in order to safeguard the essential
divinity of Christ. In the intention of St. Paul, however,
there is no ambiguity; the name describes Christ as
sovereign Lord before creation, and yet, in the mystery
of divine grace, as 'firstborn of a great brotherhood'.[5]

[1] *Op. cit.*, 147.
[2] *An Introduction to the Early History of Christian Doctrine*, 162.
[3] Cf. Moffatt, *Heb.*, 11, 'As the context indicates, the term brings out the
pre-eminent honour and the unique relationship to God enjoyed by the
Son among the heavenly host'.
[4] Cf. Bethune-Baker, *op. cit.*, 167*n*.
[5] Moffatt's translation in Rom. viii. 29.

XXXVII

THE POWER AND THE WISDOM
OF GOD

T HIS designation is applied by St. Paul to Christ
once only. It is of importance for his Christology in
view of the Jewish use of the name 'the Power' for
God and of 'the Powers' for supernatural beings. It is also
in line with the tendency to personify Wisdom in the Septuagint and later Rabbinical writings. The Apostle uses
the phrase in 1 Cor. i. 24, 'Christ the power of God, and
the wisdom of God', and in i. 30 he says that Christ was
made unto us 'wisdom from God, both righteousness and
sanctification and redemption'. Although it is far from
clear that he uses the words 'power' and 'wisdom' in a technical sense,[1] it has been widely felt that his Christology
is a 'Wisdom Christology'.[2]

Dalman[3] and others[4] have shown that in Jewish
literature ἡ δύναμις was used as a periphrasis for God, and
probably Mk. xiv. 62,[5] 'at the right hand of (the) Power',
and perhaps Ac. viii. 10,[6] 'This is the Power of God,
which is called Great', are examples of this usage. One
must hesitate to find a parallel in 1 Cor. i. 24, since St.
Paul, like St. Luke, adds 'of God', and possibly he means

[1] Cf. Robertson and Plummer, 1 *Cor.*, 23.

[2] Cf. A. E. J. Rawlinson, *The New Testament Doctrine of the Christ*,
163f., 210; C. F. Burney, *JTS*, xxvii. 160ff.

[3] *The Words of Jesus*, 200-2.

[4] Cf. Billerbeck, *Kommentar*, i. 1006f.; C. K. Barrett, *The Holy Spirit
and the Gospel Tradition*, 72; A. Richardson, *The Miracle Stories of the
Gospels*, 1-5, 16-19.

[5] Cf. V. Taylor, *The Gospel according to St. Mark*, 568.

[6] Cf. K. Lake, *The Beginnings of Christianity*, iv. 91.

only that in Christ God's mighty power has come into the world. 'The wisdom of God' is a phrase which can be explained in the same way, but here 'of God' does not call for the same interpretation, since 'wisdom' may be conceived as the medium of His revelation and rule. Moreover, Wisdom is half personified in Prov. viii. 22-31:

'The Lord possessed me in the beginning of his way,
Before his works of old.
I was set up from everlasting, from the beginning,
Or ever the earth was . . .
When he established the heavens, I was there . . .
When he marked out the foundations of the earth:
Then was I by him, as a master workman:
And I was daily his delight . . .',

and still more in Ecclesiasticus i. 1, xxiv. 3, 9:

'All wisdom cometh from the Lord,
And is with him for ever'.

'I came forth from the mouth of the Most High,
And as a mist I covered the earth'.

'He created me from the beginning, before the world;
And to the end I shall not fail',

and in passages in which Wisdom is identified with the Law, as in xix. 20:

'All wisdom is the fear of the Lord;
And in all wisdom is the fulfilling of the Law'.

Most of all is this tendency to be seen in the Alexandrian Book of Wisdom, which was probably read by St. Paul[1] and the author of the Epistle to the Hebrews,[2] and especially in the passage vii. 26, quoted earlier:[3]

'For she is an effulgence from everlasting light,
And an unspotted mirror of the working of God,
And an image of his goodness'.

[1] Cf. H. St. John Thackeray, *The Relation of St. Paul to Contemporary Jewish Thought*, 223.
[2] Cf. Moffatt, *Heb*, 6f.; Peake, *Heb*, 35.
[3] See p. 129.

L

In response to contemporary religious thought it was manifestly open to the New Testament writers to speak of Christ as 'the Wisdom of God', and probably under this influence St. Paul does so in 1 Cor. i. 24. The real question, however, is why he does not use the name more freely, especially in Col. i. 15-20, and why the author of Hebrews and St. John do not use it at all. The explanation that other names were preferred does not carry us far. The best answer yet given to the question is that 'wisdom', 'knowledge' and 'faith' had already been appropriated as sectarian watchwords by Gnostic teachers in the first century.[1] In contrast with St. John, St. Paul does not hesitate to use γνῶσις and πίστις under the strong influence of Old Testament usage, but he might well not feel the same impulse to use σοφία, particularly because of the existence of a party in Corinth which prided itself on its interest in 'wisdom' (cf. 1 Cor. i. 18-31, ii. 6-16). In naming Christ 'the Wisdom of God', he may be wresting a word from their vocabulary in a polemical situation, just as he uses πλήρωμα in Col. i. 19, and, without doubting its relevancy and truth, might not desire to use it further.[2] We are probably right in interpreting his use of the term as a tentative attempt, in special circumstances, to assign to Christ the same supramundane status which he gives to Him elsewhere in the names 'Image', 'Firstborn', and 'Last Adam'.

[1] Cf. W. F. Howard, *op. cit.*, 44.

[2] Whether St. Paul knew of Rabbinical speculations which identified Wisdom with the Torah (cf. Kittel, *KThW*, iv. 139f.), and how he would have reacted to them, we do not know. Cf. W. L. Knox, *St. Paul and the Church of the Gentiles*, 62: 'She (Wisdom) could be identified with the Torah, which could be described in the language of midrashic piety almost as a personal figure; but the Torah could never lose its character as a written book and become a real person'.

XXXVIII

THE LAST ADAM

'THE Last Adam' and 'the Second Man' are names applied to Christ by St. Paul, in antithesis to the Adam of the Genesis creation story, in Rom. v. 12-21 and I Cor. xv. 22, 45-9. This teaching has played a great role in subsequent Christian theology in connexion with the representative functions and ministry of Christ. As Adam is the head of fallen humanity, so, it has been held, Christ is the federal head of the redeemed world.

In addition to the passages mentioned above, the Markan narrative of the Temptation story may illustrate the contrast between Adam and Christ.[1] J. Jeremias[2] has worked out this contrast in some detail. As Adam was tempted, so was Christ. As Adam was revered by the wild beasts in Paradise and provided with angel's food, so Christ was 'with the wild beasts'[3] in the wilderness and ministered to by the angels. In Lk also the Genealogy, which traces the descent of Jesus from Adam, immediately precedes the Temptation story. A similar contrast has also been seen in Phil. ii. 6f. between Adam and Christ who, although in the form of God, did not think 'equality with God' a thing to be grasped. These suggestions are speculative, whereas in Rom and 1 Cor the contrast is clear.

[1] Cf. V. Taylor, *The Gospel according to St. Mark*, 164.
[2] *KThW*, i. 141-3, *Jesus als Weltvollender*, 56; A. Richardson, *TWB*, 15.
[3] Cf. Isa. xi. 6-8, lxv. 25.

In Rom. v. 14 Adam is described as 'a figure (τύπος) of him that was to come', that is, Christ. Through the one came death, through the other life; through the disobedience of Adam condemnation, through the obedience of Christ the gift of righteousness (Rom. v. 12, 17-19). Many problems, notably that of freewill, are not worked out in Rom. v. 12-21, largely because St. Paul is anxious to dwell upon the immeasurable superiority of the free gift which came to men in Christ over the judgement which fell upon them in Adam, and to insist that 'where sin abounded, grace did abound more exceedingly' (v. 20). The same contrast appears in 1 Cor. xv. 22, 'For as in Adam all die, so also in Christ shall all be made alive'. In 1 Cor. xv. 45-9 the theme of the 'spiritual body' is developed. Adapting Gen. ii. 7, the Apostle says, 'The first man Adam became a living soul', and to this he adds, 'The last Adam became a life-giving spirit' (xv. 45). 'The first man', he says, 'is of the earth, earthy: the second man is of heaven' (xv. 47); and, from these contrasting statements, he draws the inference, 'As we have borne the image of the earthy, we shall also bear the image of the heavenly' (xv. 49).

Our present concern is not with the doctrines of sin and of the resurrection with which these passages are so closely connected, but with the place they assign to Christ as the head of a redeemed humanity. 'The Last Adam' and 'the Second Man' are names which stand out even among the great Christological titles we have considered, especially 'the High Priest', 'the Image of God', 'the Firstborn', 'the Son of Man', and 'the Paraclete'. How far, and how fast, Christian thought moved from names like 'Teacher', 'Prophet', 'the Righteous One', and 'the Holy One of God'! How remote seems a name like 'Rabbi'! The driving motive in the process of doctrinal development is not exclusively intellectual; it is intellectual activity prompted by the passion of faith. The span which separates the Carpenter of Nazareth from the Second Adam, bridgeless as it might seem, is crossed in little more than twenty-five years, not by impulses from without the bounds of Christianity, but by irresistible pressure from within. Undeniably Jewish in origin, the new name had never been applied to the expected Messiah by the Jews,[1] and while we may wonder whether ancient speculations regarding Primal Man helped to provide an atmosphere for its use, the title is pre-eminently the creation of Christian faith and hope. Strange to the modern man, it contains a permanent valuation of the person of Christ.[2] Christ is not the Last Adam because He is divine; He is the Last Adam and therefore divine. Divinity is the inevitable attribute of His person and work. In the language of St. Paul, 'the Second Man is of heaven'.

[1] Cf. Billerbeck, *Kommentar*, iii. 477f; Jeremias, *op. cit.*, i. 142.
[2] See A. Nygren, *Romans*, 206-29.

XXXIX

ALPHA AND OMEGA
THE FIRST AND THE LAST
THE BEGINNING AND THE END

THESE epithets are used by the Seer John, and it is
significant that he uses them both of God and of
Christ. In i. 8 we read: 'I am the Alpha and the
Omega, saith the Lord God, which is and which was and
which is to come, the Almighty', and again in xxi. 6, 'I am
the Alpha and the Omega, the beginning and the end'. No
one who believes in God will deny the appropriateness of
these names. All the more significant, therefore, is their
application one and all to Christ. 'Fear not', says the
Glorified Christ in the opening vision of the book, 'I am
the first and the last, and the living one; and I was dead,
and behold, I am alive for evermore, and I have the keys
of death and of Hades' (i. 17f.). Similarly, the Seer is
bidden to write to the angel of the church in Smyrna,
'These things saith the first and the last, which was dead,
and lived again' (ii. 8), and at the end of the book he is
told, 'Behold, I come quickly . . . , I am the Alpha and the
Omega, the first and the last, the beginning and the end'
(xxii. 13). No names of Christ have such universality,
inclusiveness, and finality.

'The Alpha and the Omega', R. H. Charles[1] observes,
'is a natural symbol for the first and last of all things'; it
was used by the Greeks and the Romans, and later by the
Rabbis, to denote the whole extent of a thing. It may

[1] *Rev.*, i. 20.

have been a popular expression derived from Hellenistic
philosophy and mediated through Jewish teaching. The
Rabbis used it when speaking of truth as God's seal,
pointing out that of the three letters in the Hebrew word
for 'truth' *aleph* is the first letter of the alphabet, *mem* the
middle letter, and *tau* the last.[1] In fact, *mem* is the thirteenth letter in an alphabet of twenty-two letters. It
looks, therefore, as if this speculation goes back to the
Greek alphabet of twenty-four letters, of which *mu* is the
thirteenth.[2] The phrase 'the first and the last' is taken
from Isa. xli. 4, 'I the Lord, the first and with the last, I
am he', Isa. xliv. 6, 'I am the first, and I am the last; and
beside me there is no God', and Isa. xlviii. 12, 'I am he;
I am the first, I also am the last'. Charles[3] suggests that
the origins of the last phrase, 'the beginning and the end',
may be Greek, and traces it to an Orphic saying re-
corded by Plato[4] and familiar to Josephus[5] which later
was adopted by the Talmudists. There is a parallel idea
in St. Paul's reference to God in Rom. xi. 36, 'For of him,
and through him, and unto him are all things', and again
in I Cor. viii. 6, 'Of whom are all things, and we unto him',
a passage in which, with a significant change of prepos-
ition, Jesus Christ is described as the one *Kyrios* 'through
whom are all things, and we through him'. On Rom. xi.
36 Bengel's comment is, *Denotatur Origo et Cursus et
Terminus rerum omnium.* A similar thought is expressed
in Apoc. iii. 14, 'These things saith the Amen, the faithful
and true witness, the beginning of the creation of God'.[6]
The belief that the creation and consummation of all

---

[1] Cf. Kittel, *KThW*, i. 2; Charles, *op. cit.*, 20.
[2] Kittel, *ibid.*
[3] *Op. cit.*, ii. 220.
[4] *Leg.*, iv. 7.
[5] *Ant.*, viii. 11. 2.
[6] For the name 'the Amen' see p. 167f.

things are divine acts is fundamentally Biblical. The name 'the Beginning and the End' may therefore be only a variant of 'the First and the Last', and need not necessarily be Greek in origin.

Whatever may be said of the origin of these names, there can be no doubt that they illustrate the high Christology of the Apocalypse. In themselves, and because they are used both of God and of Christ, they describe a suprahuman figure who is pre-existent and beyond the bounds of time.

XL

THE BELOVED

THIS name is applied to Christ once only in Eph. i. 6, in the words, 'His grace, which he freely bestowed on us in the Beloved'. In an important note J. A. Robinson[1] argues that the name was in use as a Messianic title in New Testament times. He shows that in the Septuagint it is a title for Israel and claims that in the Gospels ὁ ἀγαπητός and ὁ ἐκλεκτός are practically interchangeable terms, and that the former is not a mere epithet of υἱός in Mk. i. 11 and ix. 7. It is difficult to suppose, he argues, that the only source of the use of 'the Beloved' in early Christian literature is Eph. i. 6. Its use also in the Ascension of Isaiah, while not pre-Christian, has verisimilitude 'in a work which affected to be a Jewish prophecy of Christ'. It cannot be said that this argument is conclusive, and on the whole it seems more probable that the name is a Christian formation prompted by Isa. v. 1, 'Let me sing for my wellbeloved a song of my beloved touching his vineyard'.

The name implies God's love for Christ, as in the parallel phrase in Col. i. 13, 'the kingdom of the Son of his love'. Here T. K. Abbott[2] is probably correct in explaining the genitive as meaning that the Son is the object of God's love. 'Love', he says, 'is not merely bestowed upon Him, but makes Him its own'.[3] Lightfoot[4] prefers

---

[1] *Eph*, 229-33.
[2] *Eph and Col*, 208
[3] *Ibid*.
[4] *Col*, 140.

159

to take the phrase as a genitive of origin which defines the Son as the revelation of the Father's love, but more recent commentators[1] agree with the view of Abbott.

The doctrine that Christ is the object of the Father's love is typically Johannine:

Jn. iii. 35:   'The Father loveth the Son, and hath given all things into his hand',

Jn. v. 20:   'For the Father loveth the Son, and showeth him all things that he himself doeth',

Jn. x. 17:   'Therefore doth my Father love me, because I lay down my life, that I may take it again',

Jn. xv. 9:   'Even as the Father hath loved me, I also have loved you',

Jn. xvii. 23f.:   'That the world may know that thou didst send me, and lovedst them, even as thou lovedst me. . . . Thou lovedst me before the foundation of the world'.

Jn. xvii. 26:   'And I made known unto them thy name, and will make it known; that the love wherewith thou lovedst me may be in them, and I in them'.

In the names 'the Beloved' and 'My beloved Son'[2] this teaching is focussed. Manifestly, their Christological significance is profound, for they imply an intimate relationship between the Father and the Son which transcends all that is true of man's communion with God.[3]

[1] Cf. Peake, *Exp. Gk. Test.*, iii. 501; Rawlinson, *Col* (Peake's *Commentary*), 868; Dibelius, *An die Kolosser Epheser an Philemon*, 6, 46.
[2] Cf. Mk. i. 11 = Mt. iii. 17 = Lk. iii. 22; Mk. ix. 7 = Mt. xvii. 5 = Lk. ix. 35; cf. Mk. xii. 6 = Lk. xx. 13; Mt. xii. 18.
[3] Cf. Lk. x. 22.

XLI

THE WORD

B Y general consent 'the Logos', or 'the Word', is one
of the greatest titles applied to Christ in the New
Testament. Many would say that it is the sub-
limest title of all. The name is used only by St. John,
in the Prologue to the Gospel, i. 1-18, and in the opening
words of the First Epistle, i. 1-4; but its ideas colour the
teaching of St. Paul in Col. i. 15-20 and of the writer of
Hebrews in Heb. i. 1-3.

The name has a long history. Used in the sixth century
B.C. by Heraclitus, and later by the Stoics, to describe the
immanent reason which pervades the universe, the term
'Logos' is frequently employed by Philo of Alexandria in
speaking of the divine reason which acts as an intermediary between God and His world. Although Philo uses
many personal names to describe the Logos, such as
'High Priest', 'Firstborn', and 'Son of God', in the last
analysis he thinks of it as an impersonal principle, and
anything like the idea of the Word becoming flesh is completely alien to his teaching.

How far the Fourth Evangelist was influenced by
Philo is much disputed.[1] Some degree of indebtedness,
direct or indirect, can hardly be denied, but other influ-

[1] Cf. E. F. Scott, *The Fourth Gospel*, 145-75; W. Sanday, *The Criticism
of the Fourth Gospel*, 185-204; B. W. Bacon, *The Fourth Gospel in Research
and Debate*, 4-9, 282; V. H. Stanton, *The Gospels as Historical Documents*,
iii. 161-86; J. E. Carpenter, *The Johannine Writings*, 290-357; J. H.
Bernard, *St. John*, xciiif., cxxxviii-cxlvii; E. C. Hoskyns, *The Fourth
Gospel*, 152-64; F. C. Burkitt, *The Church and Gnosis*, 92-100; G. Kittel,
KThW, iv. 130-40; R. H. Strachan, *The Fourth Gospel*, 90-6, 99-109;
W. F. Howard, *Christianity according to St. John*, 34-56.

ences have also played their part. Among these, with greater or less cogency, have been suggested the description of Wisdom in Prov. viii. 22-31, Sir. xxiv. 1-22, and Wisd. vii. 25ff.,[1] the identification of Wisdom with the Torah in early rabbinic speculation,[2] the Gnostic redemption-mythus,[3] and the Creation story of Gen. i., with its teaching concerning the word of God which brought order out of chaos.[4] Several scholars have suggested that the Evangelist used an earlier Hymn to the Logos in praise of Wisdom, to which he added exegetical comments.[5] That he added the Prologue after the rest of the Gospel had been written is highly probable,[6] for, while it focuses his Christology, it uses λόγος in a manner distinct from its meaning elsewhere in Jn.

In the Prologue the Word exists 'in the beginning', 'with God', and as divine (i. 1). His activity is personal, for He is the Agent in creation and the source of life and light (i. 3f.). Unknown by the world, He came to His own, but those who were His own received Him not, while as many as did receive Him were given by Him the right to become the children of God (i. 10-12). The Word, the writer declares, became flesh, and, using a verb which recalls the *Shekinah*, the visible dwelling of God among His people, he says that He 'tabernacled among us, and we beheld his glory, glory as of the only begotten

[1] See earlier, p. 151f.

[2] Cf. Billerbeck, *Kommentar*, ii. 353, 355, 357, 361, iii. 131; Kittel, *KThW*, iv. 139. The Torah is described as pre-existent, as the daughter of God, as lying on God's bosom, as the means and medium of creation, as containing words for the life of the world, and as truth.

[3] Cf. Bultmann, *Theologie*, 166, 174ff., 359f.

[4] Strachan, *op. cit.*, 90-2; Hoskyns, *op. cit.*, 152-64; Howard, *op. cit.*, 47f.

[5] Cf. J. R. Harris, *The Origin of the Prologue to St. John's Gospel;* C. F. Burney, *The Aramaic Origin of the Fourth Gospel*, 28-43; Bultmann, *Eucharisterion*, ii. 1-26.

[6] Cf. V. H. Stanton, *op. cit.*, iii. 178.

from the Father, full of grace and truth' (i. 14). The
identity of the Word is disclosed in the Baptist's testimony
in i. 15, and in i. 17, 'For the law was given by Moses;
grace and truth came by Jesus Christ'. In i. 18 the language of Sonship is used, 'No man hath seen God at any
time; the only begotten Son,[1] who is in the bosom of the
Father, he hath declared him'.

There is room for debate at what point the Prologue
begins to speak of the incarnate life of Jesus, whether at
i. 11 or i. 14,[2] but there can be little doubt that from the
first the Evangelist is thinking of Christ. It is He who
was in the beginning with God and was divine, through
whom all things were made, who came to His own and
became flesh, and whose glory was seen of men. He is
the Word, not Wisdom, not the Torah, and not any quasi-
intermediary described by the philosophers of the day.
The usage is parallel to that in which Christ is said to be
'the Truth', 'the Life', and 'the Expiation'.

It is no doubt perilous to attempt to unfold the
Evangelist's thought, when he himself has not expounded
it in detail, but it is safe to say that he is profoundly
influenced by the Genesis Creation story. In the expression 'And God said' he sees a divine activity expressing
itself in personal action. As A. R. Johnson has said of
Old Testament thought, 'the spoken word may be regarded as an effective "extension" of personality'.[3] This
conception undoubtedly gives a richer meaning to many
passages, as, for example, Psa. xxxiii. 6,

> 'By the word of the Lord were the heavens made;
> And all the host of them by the breath of his mouth',

---

[1] Probably this reading should be preferred to 'God only begotten', as
being more in harmony with the thought of the Prologue. See p. 56.

[2] O. C. Quick, *Doctrines of the Creed*, 111f., prefers to fix on i. 3f.,
'That which hath come into being *in* him was life'.

[3] *The One and the Many in the Israelite Conception of God*, 6, 20

and Psa. cvii. 20,

> 'He sendeth his word, and healeth them,
> And delivereth them from their destructions',

and still more in Isa. lv. 11, 'So shall my word be that goeth forth out of my mouth: it shall not return unto me void, but it shall accomplish that which I please, and it shall prosper in the thing whereto I sent it'.

This interpretation of 'the Word of God', however, is helpful only up to a point, for in the Old Testament 'the Word' is 'the extension' of the personality of Yahweh, whereas in the Prologue, whether the writer realised it or not, there is present a totally new conception of the being of God. He is no longer 'the high and lofty One that inhabiteth eternity, whose name is Holy' (Isa. lvii. 15), or the God who says, 'I am the Lord, and there is none else' (Isa. xlv. 6). The distinctive feature in the Prologue is that the Logos stands over against God and is Himself divine, and this conception carries with it the view that within the riches of His Being there are personal distinctions.

This perception means that, in interpreting the origin of the Johannine Logos doctrine, Christian thought will not be able to rest content permanently with the suggestiveness of Gen. i, but will be compelled to look for contributory factors in other directions, in the semi-personalised Logos of Philo, in Wisdom, in the Torah, and even, in periods of theological despair, in Gnosticism. Some vehicle of thought is necessary to bridge the gap between the Old Testament and Jn. i. 1-18. Nevertheless, it is a question of a vehicle and not of motive power. The compelling urge which led the Evangelist to pen, or make use of, the Logos Hymn, is not any of the external factors which from time to time have been proposed, but the dynamic fact of Christ Himself. It was the fact that Christ was known and worshipped in the Church of his day which drove the Evangelist to identify Him with the Word of God in his endeavour to explain His person first to himself and then to his readers. He made use of the thought forms of his day, as all the great theologians have done, and must do, to give expression to his perception of the incomparable significance of Jesus Christ. The central problems of Christology, afterwards to be debated throughout three centuries, were first raised in the atmosphere of veneration and of worship; they emerged in the catacombs and the attics of the Roman Empire.

Whether the ideas of the Prologue are to be found also in 1 Jn. i. 1-4 is a question variously answered. The majority opinion is that fundamentally they are the same, but there is a tendency to explain the phrase 'the Word of life' in 1 Jn. i. 1 in harmony with Phil. ii. 16, 'holding fast the word of life', in the sense of the Gospel.[1] There is undoubtedly a marked practical purpose manifest in this passage, a strong emphasis directed against Gnostic tendencies to insist that Christ had veritably appeared in history, and had been heard, seen, witnessed, and touched; but the phrases 'that which was from the beginning'[2] and 'which was with the Father',[3] as well as the verb 'we beheld',[4] suggest that the intellectual presuppositions are the same as those of the Prologue. The absence of the name 'the Logos' from Col. i. 15-20 and Heb. i. 1-3 must be occasioned by the same feeling which led St. Paul and the author of Hebrews to avoid the term 'the Wisdom of God', reluctance to use sectarian watchwords. St. Paul overcomes this reluctance in 1 Cor. i. 24 in the case of 'the Wisdom of God', and would probably have done so in

---

[1] Cf. C. H. Dodd, *The Johannine Epistles*, 4f.

[2] ὃ ἦν ἀπ' ἀρχῆς

[3] ἥτις ἦν πρὸς τὸν πατέρα.

[4] ἑωράκαμεν.

Colossians if the false teachers of Colossae had made play with the name 'the Word'. The writer of Hebrews prefers other names, 'Radiance', 'Image', 'Firstborn', and 'High Priest'. The Fourth Evangelist boldly appropriated the name, and thereby blazed a path which ultimately led to Nicaea.

XLII

THE AMEN

THIS name may with advantage be taken last because it sums up so much that is implied in other names and titles.

'Amen' is the transliteration of an adverb derived from a Hebrew verb which means 'to confirm', or 'to support'. In the Old Testament[1] it is used freely, with the meanings 'verily', 'truly', 'Yes', as the answer of an individual or a community to a command or word of the Lord, and it is often used in a similar way in doxologies. From the synagogue it was taken over in the worship of the first Christian assemblies. Its use as a liturgical acclamation is illustrated in 1 Cor. xiv. 16, where, in discussing the *glossolalia* at Corinth, St. Paul asks how 'the unlearned' will be able to say 'the Amen' at the giving of thanks, if he does not know what is being said; and it is implied in the Seer's descriptions of heavenly worship in the Apocalypse (v. 14, xix. 4), by his own usage (i. 6f.), and by the response, 'Amen: come, Lord Jesus', to the assurance, 'He which testifieth these things saith, Yea: I come quickly' (xxii. 20).

The Christological importance of the word is seen in 2 Cor. i. 20, where, however, it is not yet a name. 'However many soever are the promises of God', St. Paul declares, in Christ is 'the Yea'; 'wherefore also', he adds, 'through him is the Amen, unto the glory of God through

---

[1] Numb. v. 22, Deut. xxvii. 15-26, Neh. v. 13, viii. 6, 1 Chron. xvi. 36, 1 Kings i. 36, Psa. xli. 13, cvi. 48, Jer. xi. 5, xxviii. 6; 1 Esdr. ix. 47, Tob. viii. 8.

us'. Here the reference is to the Amen uttered by the
congregation in worship. It is 'through him', the Apostle
declares, that it is uttered to the glory of God. The fact
that he speaks of Christ as 'the Yea', that is, the fulfilment
of the promises, shows that it is but a step to call Him also
'the Amen'. This step is taken in Apoc. iii. 14, where the
Seer is bidden to write to the angel of the church in
Laodicea, 'These things saith the Amen, the faithful and
true witness, the beginning of the creation of God'.
Manifestly, the reference is to the Exalted Christ.
Apparently, the name was suggested by Isa. lxv. 16, 'the
God of Amen', for this may be the form in which the
Seer read the passage.[1] The Septuagint implies 'the God
of truth', which points to a different vocalisation of the
Hebrew word. One may wonder, however, whether the
characteristic use of ἀμὴν λέγω ὑμῖν in the sayings of
Jesus[2] has not contributed to the use of the word as a title.
The meaning of the name is brought out in the phrases
which follow, 'the faithful and true witness, the beginning
of the creation of God'. As 'the Amen', Christ fulfils and
attests the revelation of God. Moreover, if, as is probable,
ἀρχή in the second clause is used in the sense of αἰτία,
'cause', Christ is said to be 'the origin (or 'primary source')
of the creation of God'.[3]

The name has not entered into the Christian vocabulary
as other titles have done, but it aptly summarises the
belief of countless believers. It is of unspeakable com-
fort in seasons of doubt, and of added strength in times of
hope, to know that Christ is 'the Amen' to all the assur-
ances of God.

[1] Cf. Charles, *Rev.* i. 94.
[2] In Mk 13 times, in Mt 30, in Lk 6, and in the double form 25 times
in Jn. H. Schleier, *KThW*, i. 341, affirms that in this 'Amen' the whole of
Christology is contained *in nuce*.
[3] So Charles, *ibid.* Cf. Swete, *The Apocalypse of St. John*, 58f.

CONCLUDING SUMMARY

THE dominating impression we receive from a close study of the names and titles of Jesus is that of their number, variety, and Christological importance. In all, some fifty-five names have been examined; and, while about twenty of them may be said to have had a temporary vogue, the rest have established themselves in the Christian vocabulary and are in constant use down to the present day.

An outstanding feature is the steady replacement of purely Messianic names by those with a societary or communal significance. Equally important are the soteriological names. Christian thought has found it natural to embody its sense of the person of Christ in names which describe His work. The Christological names in the proper sense of the term have freely entered into the stream of theological discussion, and they are especially valuable because they sum up in a name what is, in reality, a process of thought, all the more impressive because in most cases it is not consciously pursued, and because it is compounded of elements derived from personal devotion and liturgical usage.

It will be of advantage to distinguish three periods, to which the various names belong, in order to see more exactly when they first emerged and to what extent they persisted or fell by the way.

The first period is obviously that covered by the historic ministry. The second period extends from A.D. 30 to 65. It coincides with the first generation of the Christian Mission, and is represented by the Gospels, the Acts, and

the Epistles of St. Paul. The third period is that of the
second generation, extending from A.D. 65 to 100, to
which 1 Peter, the Epistle to the Hebrews, and the Johannine writings belong, and which is represented in its later
phases by the Catholic and Pastoral Epistles, and, with a
strong admixture of primitive elements, by the Apocalypse of St. John.

The names which emerge in the earliest period, that of
the Ministry of Jesus, include 'Jesus', 'the Son of Joseph',
'Rabbi', 'Rabboni', 'the Teacher', 'the Master', 'Prophet',
'the Christ', 'the Son of David', 'the Son of Man', 'the Son
of God', 'the Son', 'His Son', 'My Beloved Son', 'the
King', 'He that Cometh', 'the Holy One of God', 'the
Bridegroom', 'the Shepherd'—nineteen in all. Of these
those which passed out of general use after the Resurrection are 'Rabbi', 'Rabboni', 'the Teacher', ' Prophet',
'the Son of Joseph', 'the Son of David', 'My Beloved Son',
'He that Cometh', 'the Holy One of God', 'the Master'
(except is so far as it has re-appeared in modern times) and
'the Son of Man', which lingered for a while in Palestinian
circles (cf. Ac. vii. 56) and was a theme of theological
interest in the Church at Ephesus. From this period,
therefore, we are left with eight names, which continued
to be used through New Testament times and have
become the permanent possession of the Church; they
are 'Jesus', 'Christ', 'the Son of God', 'the Son',
'His Son', 'the King', 'the Bridegroom', and 'the
Shepherd'.

In the period from A.D. 30 to 65 the names 'the King',
'the Shepherd', and 'the Bridegroom' are temporarily in
eclipse, but 'Jesus', 'Christ', 'the Son of God', 'the Son',
and 'His Son', and various combinations of these names,
are in constant use. In addition, the following are found:
'the Prophet', 'the Servant', 'the Lord', 'the Righteous

One', 'the Judge', 'the Stone', 'the Head of the Body', 'the Image of God', 'the Power and the Wisdom of God', 'the Firstborn', 'the Last Adam', 'the Beloved'. Of these twelve the use made of 'the Prophet', 'the Servant', 'the Righteous One', 'the Power and the Wisdom of God', and 'the Beloved' is limited and occasional; whereas 'the Lord', by itself and in the names 'the Lord Jesus', 'the Lord Jesus Christ', and 'Our Lord Jesus Christ', is the most common designation of all. The single instance of the name 'the Beloved' breathes a devotional atmosphere, and the names 'the Judge', 'the Stone', and 'the Head of the Body' serve hortatory as well as doctrinal ends. The remaining names, 'the Image of God', 'the Power and the Wisdom of God', 'the Firstborn', and 'the Last Adam' are Pauline and theological. They are tentative attempts, in response to practical needs, to describe the significance of Christ's person, and are additional to the common confession of primitive Christianity, in which St. Paul fervently joins, that Jesus is 'the Son of God'. Of immense importance for the subsequent development of theology, they are less numerous and less frequently employed than is commonly supposed. The theological interest is undoubtedly emerging and growing in strength during this period, but, contrary to what has often been assumed, it is still far outweighed by liturgical, devotional, and practical motives. As the facts concerning the use of *Kyrios* show to the point of demonstration, the creative theological work of the period was done in an atmosphere of veneration and worship. Men thought upon their knees; and so far from the worship being a distorting element, it was stimulating and creative. It is highly significant that architecture in the middle ages and theology in the first century had a common inspiration in thanksgiving, praise, and prayer.

The period A.D. 65 to 100 entered into a great legacy. It inherited from the days of the Ministry the names 'Jesus', 'Christ', 'the Son of God', 'the Son', 'His Son', 'the King', 'the Bridegroom', and 'the Shepherd', and brought the last three again into the foreground. From the second period it took over the names 'the Prophet', 'the Lord', 'the Judge', 'the Stone', 'the Image', 'the Firstborn', 'the Saviour', but with only a limited use of the first name in Jn. Its distinctive feature is the wide extent to which it expanded its inheritance. From the Epistle to the Hebrews it gained the names 'the Pioneer', 'the Radiance', 'the Mediator', and 'the High Priest'; from the Fourth Gospel the seven 'I am' sayings, with the names 'the Bread of Life', 'the Light of the World', 'the Door of the Sheep', 'the Good Shepherd', 'the Resurrection and the Life', 'the True Vine', and 'the Way, and the Truth, and the Life', and, in addition, 'the Lamb of God' and 'the Word'; and from 1 Jn the descriptive phrases 'the Paraclete' and 'the Expiation'. In the Catholic and Pastoral Epistles the period found new meaning in the name 'the Saviour'. Finally, from the Apocalypse of St. John it received short-lived Messianic names like 'the Lion of the Tribe of Judah', 'the Root and Offspring of David', 'the Bright and Morning Star', a fuller use of the name 'the Lamb', and the designations 'the Alpha and the Omega', 'the First and the Last', 'the Beginning and the End', and the summary name 'the Amen'.

Again one cannot fail to be conscious of the debt the period owed to Christ-mysticism and to worship. From religious devotion came the imperishable names in the Johannine sayings; from worship a recrudescence of Messianic terms, the use of 'the Alpha and the Omega' and its equivalents, the name 'the Lamb', and the phrase 'the Amen' in the Seer's descriptions of the psalmody of heaven. It derived also an increased use of the name 'the Saviour' from primitive Christian hymns embedded in the later Epistles. Indeed, if we isolate the names which manifest a primary intellectual interest to express the Christological significance of Jesus, the list is relatively short. It includes, in the Epistle to the Hebrews, the titles 'the Pioneer', 'the Mediator', 'the High Priest', 'the Express Image', and 'the Radiance of the Divine Glory', and in the Johannine writings 'the Paraclete', 'the Expiation', and 'the Word'. Of course, we must add to these names 'the Son of God', 'the Son', 'His Son', handed down from the primitive tradition, and the name 'the Only Begotten Son' used by St. John, and we must recognise the immense theological importance of these names, especially that of 'the Word'. Nevertheless, it remains true of this period, as of the period A.D. 30 to 65, that liturgical and devotional interests are as strongly operative as the doctrinal impulse. In particular, the sacramental convictions of the Fourth Evangelist are reflected in the names 'the Bread of Life' and 'the True Vine', while, as we have seen, the name 'the Lord' was closely associated with Baptism and the Eucharist.

The importance of the names and titles of Jesus is now, I hope, sufficiently apparent. It would not be possible from these alone to expound a doctrine of the Person of Christ, for the names cannot be dissociated in the mind from the fuller teaching of the New Testament writers; but we can certainly say that the names focus the teaching and express what was believed and taught. They are the signs and seals of the earliest Christology, and by their subsequent use throughout the centuries the Church has endorsed their permanent validity.

A striking confirmation of this claim is the fact that the
Church has never been able to add other names in any
significant degree. The one exception is the name 'the
Redeemer'. The absence of this name from the New
Testament, in spite of the fact that it uses the correspond-
ing verbs,[1] and despite the striking use of the name in the
Old Testament,[2] is somewhat of an enigma. It may be
that its basic meaning, 'the Vindicator', did not commend
its use to the New Testament writers. More probably its
absence is to be explained by the fact that it lacked that
depth of meaning which subsequently Christianity poured
into it.[3] If so, Christian usage has enriched the word
'redeemer' with meaning derived from the Gospel itself.
No other new name is comparable with it. Moreover, the
number of new names is surprisingly small. If we set
aside descriptive phrases in the Creeds and borrowed
names in hymns, we are left with such designations as
'The Man of Sorrows', 'Our Blessed Lord', 'Our Dear
Lord', 'the Great Galilean', 'the Master', 'the Elder
Brother', 'the Carpenter of Nazareth'. The list is not
impressive. Indeed, it is as depressing as a group of raw,
self-conscious recruits. For the most part the new names
are either pietistic or humanistic, laudatory or non-
committal. Uninspired, they say too much or too little.
The classic names are those of the New Testament, 'the
Lord', 'the Son', 'the Word', 'Jesus', 'Jesus Christ', 'Our
Lord Jesus Christ', and they are the only names with a

---

[1] Ἀγοράζω in Apoc. v. 9, xiv. 3, 4; ἐξαγοράζω in Gal. iii. 13, iv. 5;
and λυτρόω in Lk. xxiv. 21, Tit. ii. 14, 1 Pet. i. 18.

[2] Job. xix. 25, Psa. xix. 14, lxxviii. 35, Prov. xxiii. 11, Isa. xli. 14,
xliii. 14, xliv. 6, 24, xlvii. 4, xlviii, 17, xlix. 7, 26, liv. 5, 8, lix. 20, lx. 16,
lxiii. 16, Jer. i, 34. In most of these passages the participles ὁ λυτρούμενος
and ὁ ῥυσάμενος are used.

[3] λυτρωτής is not a classical word. In the LXX it appears twice only
in Psa. xviii. (xix.) 14 and lxxvii. (lxxviii.) 35. In the single New Testament example in Ac. vii. 35 it describes Moses as the deliverer of Israel.

foreseeable future. This fact is one of the neglected arguments for the plenary inspiration of Holy Scripture, and a vindication of the claim that the examination of the names and titles is a necessary prelude to the study of the Person of Christ.

INDEX OF PROPER NAMES

PRINTED IN GREAT BRITAIN
BY ROBERT MACLEHOSE AND CO. LTD
THE UNIVERSITY PRESS, GLASGOW

Date Due

DEMCO NO 295

CANISIUS

PAID

NOV 18 '72

NOV 22 1999

DEC 18 1999

CANISIUS

PAID '63

PAID CANISIUS